SPIRITUAL
CAPITALISM

How 9/11 gave us
nine spiritual lessons
of work and business

Peter Ressler
Monika Mitchell Ressler

Foreword by Marc Gunther

Spiritual Capitalism
By Peter Ressler and Monika Mitchell Ressler

Published by:
Chilmark Books | 243 Fifth Avenue, #227 | New York, NY 10016
(212) 741-1748

Cover Photo by Monika Mitchell Ressler © 2007
Edited by Cierra Trenery
Cover Design by Monika Mitchell Ressler with Bob Aucilino

 Printed on recycled paper

Publisher's Cataloging-in-Publication
(Provided by Quality Books, Inc.)

Ressler, Peter.
    Spiritual capitalism : how 9/11 gave us nine spiritual lessons of
  work and business
  / written by Peter Ressler & Monika Mitchell Ressler. --
  Rev. ed.
    p. cm.
    LCCN 2005938735
    ISBN 0-9761984-2-8
    ISBN 0-9761984-0-1
    ISBN 0-9761984-1-X

    1. Business--Religious aspects. 2. Capitalism--Moral
  and ethical aspects. 3. Social responsibility of
  business. 4. Spiritual life. I. Ressler, Monika
  Mitchell. II. Title.

HF5388.R47 2006   174'.4
          QBI06-600014

This book is dedicated to the
Fire Department of the City of New York.

We will never forget...

◆

For The Angels Among Us

Father Mychal Judge, OFM, former Chaplain of the FDNY, and Captain Patrick Brown and the other 341 firefighters who lost their lives saving lives on September 11, 2001

♦

For Spiritual Capitalists

The late Michael Mortara, former Partner-in-Charge of Global Fixed Income at Goldman Sachs, and Tom Tucker, former Managing Director of Global Fixed Income Sales at Lehman Brothers and Founder of The Fiver Foundation

Acknowledgements

We would like to thank Father Christopher Keenan, OFM, Chaplain of the FDNY, for his continuing spiritual inspiration. Our deep gratitude to NYC Firefighters Mark Gentile, Lt. Anthony Mauro, Tim "Smitty" Smith and the members of the "Big House" in Rockaway, Queens; Peter Zuck formerly of Engine 14; Sal Scarentino, Jimmy Duffy, Mike Yarembinsky, Steve Wojckchowski and the remaining members of Engine 1, Ladder 24; and the rest of the Fire Department of the City of New York, for showing us the true meaning of courage and compassion.

We are forever grateful to Marc Gunther for the selfless gift of his time, talent and support to this book. He is a man of honor and ethics as true as any firefighter in these pages.

We would like to say a special and heartfelt thanks to retired FDNY Captain Al Fuentes (www.the-patriot-group. org) whose humility and passion for helping fellow firefighters continues to inspire us. We would also like to thank retired FDNY Firefighter Tim Brown (www.thebravest.com) for all of his wonderful support for our work. We want to acknowledge active FDNY Captain Dan Sheridan (www.mutual-aid. org) for sharing his dedication to firefighters everywhere.

Many friends have contributed in a big way to this work including our very dear friend, the late Barbara Ivacek, without whose guidance, encouragement, and love this book would never have been published. Words cannot express our thanks to another dear friend and angel on earth, Constance Messmer, who has helped us tremendously on our spiritual path and through that given us the greatest gift in our life.

We cannot thank enough the exceptionally gifted and dedicated, Kathleen Loughery, who has contributed invaluable wisdom and guidance to our cause.

Our spiritual brother and advisor, Mark Sclafani, has contributed so much to our lives and towards this publication with his wise words, unlimited support, love and friendship. Our dear friend and colleague, Ron Davison, is as close to a saint as anyone we know. We are indebted forever to him for his endless patience and dedication to our business and lives.

We want to acknowledge the support of our dear friend Norman Toy for his boundless wisdom and friendship. Another dear friend, NYPD Officer and volunteer firefighter, George Bodenmiller continues to inspire us with his loyalty and love throughout this process.

Our friend and financial advisor, Abed Mansoor of Broder Mansoor, has served as a living example of spiritual capitalism. Our colleague and friend, Jim Mirenda has contributed his never-ending enthusiasm and support for our work.

Spiritual capitalist, J-Robert Ouimet, PhD, has provided inspiration and support for these ideas. Judi Neal, PhD, founder of Spirit at Work has donated her wonderful joy and enthusiasm to our project. Other members of ASAW deserve a special mention and thanks for their support: Shiela Wall, Debbie Italiano, Tim Shea and Lynda Klau.

Many people in our professional life have gone out of their way to support this work and have become friends in the process. We wish to thank the talented editor and writer, David

Zweig of the World Business Academy, for continuing to support and assist us with our message. We could not possibly thank the brilliant David Javdan enough or express our gratitude for all he has done on our behalf and continues to do.

Ann Bassett of Bunch of Grapes, Vineyard Haven, Massachusetts has given us the gift of her time, professional advice and friendship for this work.

Marci Koblenz of Companies-That-Care has become a friend and colleague in our shared vision of the future of business.

Tom Tucker and Bill Griffin of the Fiver Foundation (www.fiver.org) have provided real-life inspiration for these concepts.

Thanks also to Bill Manger, Miguel Centeno, and Jose Sifontes of the New York Chapter of the Small Business Association for their support for our work.

We wish to mention dear friend and advisor, Sara Denning, PhD, whose wisdom and help has kept us sane through this process and who continues to be an important part of our lives.

Other friends and colleagues have proved invaluable resources in the development of this work. Dr. Anthony Caliendo, Dr. Donna Mutter, Dr. Fred Kingsbury, Elaine Abrams, Anna Girandola, Genevieve Girandola, Lou Vuolo, Saniel Bonder, Marie Eisele, Elaine Mattingly, Trudy Beers, David Arnold, Professor Jim Stoner, Helena Steiner-Hornsteyn, Sharon Hamilton, Sheldon and Halina Hughes, Barbara Stahura, Eric and Edith Mayer, John Bogard, Sandy Babey and Paolo Cappoci, Ellen, Dean and Miriam Sulpy have supplied encouragement and assistance in keeping our book alive. Thanks to Professor Wyan Evans for providing help in our research.

We could not have produced this current edition without the extraordinary talent and efforts of Warwick Associates in Sonoma, California. Simon Warwick-Smith dropped out of heaven and with Kate Warwick-Smith and Cierra Trenery, they have created "The Dream Team" for any author. We are forever grateful for their invaluable expertise, advice, assistance and patience in refining this work.

The following firefighters have provided inspiration by their living example of purpose and passion: Chief Tom Farrell, Chief Joe Marino, Commissioner Fred Herrmann, Commissioner Tom Butler and the rest of the Islip, New York Volunteer Fire Department, who taught both of us what it means to be a firefighter.

A special thanks to retired firefighter Bruce Schalk, Engine 255, Ladder 157, for showing Peter his first glimpse of a firefighter's dedication when he saved his life twenty-three years ago.

Thanks also to the brotherhood in our New Jersey community and for the unlimited dedication and selfless support of Chief Kevin Saharic, Assistant Chief Al Bross and 18 Fire of Lebanon, New Jersey and Chief Peter Melick, Assistant Chief John Melick and 24 Fire of Oldwick, New Jersey.

We offer a special thanks to our colleagues and friends on Wall Street who embody the principles set forth in these pages: Pete Briger, Jimmy Tammaro, Evan Wein, Steve Mnuchin, Martin Shafiroff, Roger Gordon, Richard Johnson, Joe McGrath, Rick Van Zijl, Scott Lawin, Bobby Cagnina, Bob Christie, Peter Feinberg, Rob Incorvaia, John Urban, Pat Dealy, Jonathan Savitz, James Kase, Lori Ostenfeld, Bob O'Shea, Nancy Hament, Tom Daniels and Steve Gula.

We want to thank family members who have made our path easier by their continuing support: George and Joan Call, Edyth Ressler and Robert Mitchell. With love and thanks to Sandy Ressler for his larger-than-life presence on earth and in heaven.

Our three beautiful children have helped make this project possible with their loving encouragement and support and we thank them for their continued blessing in our lives.

And last but not least, we are forever grateful to the late "Doc" Blumenthal and the Honorable Peter W. Mitchell who planted the seeds for this book many years ago by the example of their lives.

◆

"Everybody's doing it."

"It just doesn't seem right.
I'm making enough
money without it."

CONVERSATION REGARDING

QUESTIONABLE PRICING OF TRADES

Table of Contents

"The problems of this world cannot possibly be solved by skeptics or cynics whose horizons are limited by the obvious realities. We need men who can dream of things that never were."

JOHN F. KENNEDY

AMERICAN PRESIDENT

Foreword

By Marc Gunther

Fortune Staff Writer and
Author of *Faith and Fortune*

WHERE were you on September 11, 2001? I bet you remember. I was in Los Angeles, on assignment for *Fortune* magazine, where I've worked as a writer since 1996. I rented a car and drove to Yahoo, the big Internet portal which immediately became a place where people congregated, virtually, to connect with friends and family, to share emotions and to donate money. The people who work at Yahoo were really excited. They felt like they were making a difference, albeit from a distance.

To Peter Ressler and his wife of fourteen years, Monika Mitchell Ressler, the terrorist attack was much more personal. Peter and Monika had worked on Wall Street as partners in their own executive search firm for ten years, on assignment for big investment banks like Goldman Sachs and Lehman Brothers. Peter and their older son were in Manhattan when the planes hit. Monika and their younger son were in suburban Long Island. They had friends in the investment world who died. They also had friends among the New York City firefighters who responded to the emergency. Monika had hired firefighters, on their days off, to renovate commercial and residential investment properties, a business she ran on the side. Peter had been friends for many years with Father Mychal Judge, the New York City Fire Department chaplain, who was the first official casualty of the attack. Peter and Monika were intimately familiar with the two groups of people who collided that day—the privileged Wall Street executives and the working-class firefighters who poured into the Twin Towers in an effort to save them.

We all admired the firefighters, of course. They were brave. They were modest. They suffered without complaining. They became the heroes of the city, celebrated at a rock concert in Madison Square Garden, cheered every night at Yankee Stadium.

Yes, we admired them. But some of us, I dare say, were a little jealous as well—not of the risks they take, or of the rigors of the job, or of its occasional tedium. No, we were jealous because the fire fighters believed so strongly in what they were doing. Their work had value. It had meaning. It had purpose. It had nobility. They inspired the rest of us, at least for a while.

Remarkable things happened after September 11. Americans reached out across class and racial divides to help one another. A multimillionaire financial advisor sat down with the widows of the waiters and busboys who died in Windows on the World, a posh restaurant atop one of the towers, to ask, "How can I help?" As Peter and Monika write, "People by the millions were so moved by the suffering of strangers that for a brief period of time, they put aside their own needs and thought only of others. Surely in this we saw grace."

Sadly, too many people went back to business as usual after a while. Old habits die hard. The months and years that followed brought corporate scandals: Enron, Worldcom, Tyco and the rest. Wall Street was implicated, too. Conventional thinking reasserted itself. As Peter puts it, "We have been taught to separate our hearts from what we do in business. Business is supposed to be a cold, calculating numbers game." The lessons of September 11—the hope and the bonds that it sparked, that feeling that we were all connected to one another had been forgotten.

Fortunately, Peter and Monika have not forgotten. They have given us the wonderful gift of this book, which is about what the New York City fire department has to teach Wall Street, and the rest of us, about money and business and work.

To be sure, Peter and Monika are idealists. They believe that there's a better way to do business—a way that is caring, generous and loving. They believe that business, done right, can be a noble pursuit. They believe that nice guys can finish first. And remember—these are people who have worked on Wall Street for years.

I happen to believe they are right. As a reporter who has covered corporate America for a decade, I am encouraged by the changes I've seen. Better leaders. Companies that are more caring and compassionate, more diverse, more green, more transparent. Not all of them, of course, but many.

Spiritual Capitalism is a rare book that delivers both good news and good advice: All of us can bring the same passion and purpose to our work that the rescue workers did to theirs on September 11. Indeed, we owe ourselves—and each other—nothing less.

◆

Preface

THROUGH the trials and tribulations of the twentieth century, we have come to the conclusion that capitalism is the most highly functioning economic system we have. Despite its practicality, there remain large gaping holes of inequity in its modern practice. The ruthless and vicious American capitalism of the past is crying out for change in our modern world. The question for many of us is, "What can we do about this?"

While governments, economists and experts of all kinds struggle with this question, individually we feel frustrated. How can any one person make a change in this complicated web of profiteering? In the pages that follow we describe how every one of us can and needs to be part of the change.

Spiritual Capitalism is about the spirit of each of us in business. Our concepts transcend individual religious or political platforms and reach into the humanity of us all. We offer a unique voice in the human search for a better way. The following pages are filled with new ways of looking at old ideas along with observations and solutions that have never before been said. The nine lessons take the heady concepts of institutionalized capitalism and make them personal for each of us. Because in the end, everything in our lives, including our business affairs, is personal.

Spiritual Capitalism offers an easy-to-understand portrayal of how money and business work in our lives. It makes these concepts real and translates them into everyday language that anyone can understand. This book is for all of us who work for a living and need money to live. *Spiritual Capitalism* may not answer all of your questions, but we hope we have answered many of them. The rest is up to you, individually and collectively, to make these changes a basic part of your business life.

—*Peter and Monika Ressler*

> *"I believe the power to make money is a gift from God... to be developed and used to the best of our ability for the good of mankind."*
>
> JOHN D. ROCKEFELLER
> BUSINESS MOGUL

Roots of Spiritual Capitalism

IN July 2001, we read an article in *Fortune* magazine called "God and Business" written by the renowned journalist, and author of this book's foreword, Marc Gunther. It detailed the spiritual practices of various CEOs and how these were included in their business affairs. The story set us on fire. We had been working for some time on a manuscript about business ethics, but had been careful not to shatter what has been called the "last taboo" in business. In business, and Wall Street especially, there is a clear line that separates money from more "personal" matters. Spiritual life and anything having to do with loftier goals rarely enter the business world. After all, business is not personal. For years we followed this belief—hook, line and sinker—like everyone else. Even after Gunther's article appeared we did not cross that line. Yet this story in a major business publication proved to us that others had the same yearning we did—to find deeper meaning in their work and business lives. It created a new and passionate dialogue between us: "Why *would* we leave our soul out of business? How *could* we separate ourselves like that?"

Two months later when the September 11 tragedy directly hit our business and lives, we put our manuscript on the shelf as we put our lives back together. When we picked it up again a year later, we understood through the death and destruction we had just witnessed how spirituality and business were related. Our spiritual life was crucial in rebuilding our business. Our personal and business lives were thoroughly intertwined in the aftermath of the tragedy, as we recognized the opposing forces of the self-sacrificing code of firefighting and the self-serving code of business. Suddenly we had a new sense of urgency—a calling, if you will—to put down in words the powerful revelations we had experienced through that fateful year. Were we in the middle of all this for a reason? Had we survived to tell our story for a purpose greater than ourselves? There was no time to waste. As one close friend and New York firefighter put it, "You never know how much time you have left." Our cautiousness was replaced by a newfound courage to speak out—inspired by the seemingly limitless courage of the New York firefighters that surrounded us.

When our first edition was released in 2005, a fifty-nine-year-old multimillionaire, supermarket chain owner and personal friend mentioned that the title, *Spiritual Capitalism*, confused him initially. As a practicing Catholic, this man considers himself spiritual. He is also a maverick of compassionate capitalist practices in his business. We pointed out to him that he was a spiritual capitalist and *spiritual*, as we used the term, meant *of the soul*. We asked what his objection was to this title if it represented him so accurately. He said these were two words that were never used together. Therefore, he couldn't understand what we meant by the title. We explained that is precisely why we coined the phrase—to put these two words together.

We use the term *spiritual capitalism* to differentiate it from the practice of traditional capitalism. We call our platform spiritual because our ideas are concerned with the deepest part of ourselves, the connection between the mind and heart where we make our most personal moral decisions. For some of you with a strong religious practice or faith, the term spiritual requires little further explanation. For others who do not rely on a religion or faith, spiritual can be defined as all that is connected to your higher self. In this sense, the term spiritual refers to your sense of justice, compassion and ethical conscience—the part of yourself that is concerned with things beyond your own needs. Each of us is culpable in business for its outcome. Each of us is responsible for how our actions affect others in any area of our lives. Our business lives are no exception.

For some, eyes glaze over when the term spiritual is used. They mistakenly assume a dogmatic religious aspect to anything spiritual. Ironically, we derived the phrase spiritual capitalism after hearing a colleague state, "I am an atheist, but I attend my (Unitarian) church for my spiritual life." We concluded that everyone has a spiritual life. Religious doctrine can easily mask unspiritual agendas as we know from our experiences on September 11. While religion in the case of others, like Father Mychal Judge (the first official casualty of 9/11), can reveal a deep spiritual integrity. Therefore, those who hold a genuine religious calling and those who hold simply a moral one can find practical purpose in the principles of spiritual capitalism.

In all of us, our spirituality exists beyond our physical and material selves. Some individuals understand this through a connection with a supreme intelligence. For others, this manifests as an awareness of your connection with people and things outside of yourself. Our spiritual growth culminates in a desire to find deeper meaning to our daily lives. For the purpose of this book, we focus on the spiritual part of ourselves that desires greater meaning in our work.

The Search for Truth

The subject of our personal spirituality has come up over the last couple of years, since the first edition of this book was released. We did not address this issue in that volume. For purposes of background information, I include it now, though it is not a simple answer. Our spiritual path has been a complicated route, taking many detours and encompassing several different faiths.

Peter is of Russian Jewish heritage. His great-grandparents immigrated to the United States in the late nineteenth century, probably to escape pogroms and persecution—he is not sure. His Judaism was denied to him as his parents renounced their faith before he was born and raised him a Christian Scientist. His earliest memories include practitioners praying over him at the first sign of a cold. He never went to a medical doctor as a child and practiced "mind over body" meditations long before they were commonplace. He recalls being the only kid in his all-Jewish neighborhood in Flatbush, Brooklyn with a Christmas tree. At the age of twelve, he was asked to make a personal commitment to Christian Science. He declined and spent the next decade or so as an angry young man only to find renewed spirituality within the walls of Alcoholics Anonymous. When we met in 1991, he often described how his Higher Power had saved his life.

I was baptized Presbyterian and grew up believing Jesus walked at my side. My father renounced the Greek Orthodoxy of his parents and my mother the Lutheranism of her Nazi Germany youth, and joined the local Methodist church. I assisted my pastor in teaching Sunday school until he lost patience with my questioning the literal translation of the Bible. The spiritual challenge of my mother's alcoholism urged me to rebel. My father's solution was to send me to a Catholic convent for my fifteenth year. I spent my brief time there memorizing the Rosary, studying French and shooting skeet.

At sixteen, I kept my connection to the Holy Spirit and left the convent and everything else behind. I began practicing transcendental meditation and reading books by Jung, Emerson and the Dalai Lama. After singing together in the church choir for many years, my mother chose the day of my father's death to confess her atheism to me. Three months and three days later, she took her own life. In turn, her passing ended my faith in God. In my naiveté, I believed God had forsaken me. After seven dark years of the soul, my search culminated in a profound awakening and renewed faith.

Peter and I have journeyed together these past fourteen years as husband and wife. We have raised two children from his first marriage and one from our own, created a successful business, and together experienced an extraordinary spiritual epiphany. The result is he teaches me how we can create anything with thought, and I show him how compassion is his greatest strength. Our spiritual paths have paralleled our professional paths until they finally intersected in September 2001.

Breaking the Taboo

In the past year and a half since our first publication, *Spiritual Capitalism: What the FDNY Taught Wall Street About Money*, we have received enthusiastic responses from individuals from all aspects of the business and working worlds that are truly on fire from the concepts herein. Billionaire CEOs, Wall Street executives and businesspeople of all kinds have embraced these concepts with comments like, "This is timely and necessary." Working people have sighed relief and said, "Finally!" One investment banking executive called our book "a landmark on Wall Street." People have expressed excitement over a new practice of capitalism that includes humanity in its bottom line. From this overwhelming response, we have confirmed our belief that people in business are searching for a new path. We no longer desire to work for money alone. There is a growing spiritual hunger to find a deeper connection between our souls and our work. The business community is yearning for a new code of behavior to replace an historic absence of ethics. Honest executives are sick and tired of a handful of individuals destroying the trust they have worked many years to protect. Business no longer wants to be seen as the enemy. It is bad business to be mistrusted by those whose support is crucial to our profit.

In response, a powerful force of integrity-minded businesspeople has emerged. We are part of this. With this book, we are breaking a taboo that is no longer useful in order to connect our personal selves with business.

Naming Names

Some have asked us why we purposely omit "real names" in the stories that follow. Much of the information and examples throughout this book have been gathered through years of business and personal confidences. We cannot betray that trust. For us, however, the names of individuals are irrelevant to the purpose of spiritual capitalism. Our aim is not to vilify anyone. We do not wish to position ourselves as moral judges over others. Anyone practicing every-man-for-himself capitalism is simply doing what he or she has been taught. As far back as anyone can remember, the motto from business school has been "Cash is King." Our goal is to inspire individuals to another possibility of a more humane practice of capitalism.

Our literary agent in New York and a couple of well-known publishers suggested we remove references to the firefighters and the September 11 tragedy, as this was "old news." We concluded that the examination of human tragedy is never "old." After all, the countless stories of the Holocaust, and other historical human tragedies, never fail to move us. Like any other extreme event in our lives, the tragedy of 9/11 can serve as our teacher. In America, it is the pivotal event of the twenty-first century. It has changed everything for us, right down to the way we think. In this time of global economies and instant information, when America changes, it has huge implications for the world. We can use our memories and suffering from this enormous tragedy as a catalyst for change. Peter and I have personally gleaned something positive from this horror: a new way of working.

Spiritual Capitalism asks each of us to question our own contribution to the current economic climate. Personally we have a great deal of faith in the basic honor code of individuals—more faith perhaps than people deserve, we have been told. "Isn't that Pollyanna?" queried one talk show host when we spoke of "capitalism with a conscience." We replied, "Not any more than any other moral code we might have." Is faithfulness to one's spouse "Pollyanna"? Clearly, human beings are as prone to infidelity as they are to greed. Why should we expect anything less from our business community than we do of ourselves?

People Don't Change

As we travel the country, our listeners and audiences relay how they are heartened that two executives from one of the most cutthroat arenas of business, Wall Street headhunting, have taken the time and effort to speak about a more compassionate capitalism. Cynicism however is a real human reaction to any new idea or ideal. At a lecture in an affluent Northeastern vacation community, an ex-Wall Street analyst asked us, "How can you get people to change? People don't change." The mood of the angry public over corporate impropriety is forcing business to change. When humane capitalism becomes a social dictate among the general public, even people who do not want to change will be forced to for fear of isolation. If we create a taboo against unethical and destructive acts of greed, others will follow suit. Some will understand it is "the right thing to do." Others who do not wish to be ostracized will behave in socially acceptable ways whether they believe in it or not.

Yet how possible is it really for people to change? When we look back in history over the relatively short span of years since the creation of America, we recognize a great deal of social and economic change. While social changes (abolishing slavery, voting, labor and civil rights) bring about economic change, economic changes (industrialization, technological advancement) also bring about social change. These social and economic issues go hand in hand. Currently our culture is in the middle of huge technological and social changes. We are moving from a national economy to a global one, largely due to major advances in modern technology. Our moral codes cannot adapt at the same speed that technology is expanding. We are constantly reexamining our ethical viewpoint with each new invention.

The Good Old Days

In the early days of our nation, a large portion of our economy was based on slave ownership. Individuals profited at the expense of the personal liberty and dignity of fellow human beings. It is hard to imagine that less than 200 years ago ordinary "law-abiding" American citizens justified profiting in this way. Survival-of-the-fittest Darwinism was inserted into capitalism by the English philosopher Herbert Spencer and embraced by economic warriors like Andrew Carnegie. This perspective gave Carnegie, Rockefeller and revered businessmen of their time *carte blanche* in their pursuit of profit. "Anything goes" capitalism was the modus operandi for financial success a mere century ago. At the end of the nineteenth century, the American economy was controlled by a handful of indifferent capitalists glibly known as robber barons. Moguls like Jay Gould, the "little wizard of Wall Street," openly paid lawmakers to pass legislation that boosted his personal profits and claimed he did so for the public good. Price-fixing, currency manipulations, production monopolies and worker exploitation were common and accepted practices. From our twenty-first-century view, these acts seem like unbridled gluttony and corruption. Yet in the late 1880s most of these activities were legal. It was the public response to these excesses that forced business to change. Gradually the public called for limits on how we profit by outlawing practices like child labor and establishing guidelines for working hours and minimum wage. Remarkably, these changes occurred less than seventy years ago with the 1938 Fair Labor Standards Act.

Yet change we did with the social evolution of the twentieth-century mind. Our economic progress can be seen easily when we compare nineteenth-century business to the present. While Carnegie Steel thrived on the cruel abuse of its workers, a mere hundred years later a comparable industry giant, Microsoft, consistently makes the Fortune's "100 Best Companies to Work For" list. Business has progressed to reflect our modern values. Perhaps at the end of this century, the current business culture will be viewed as unenlightened as we now see our Gilded Age forbearers.

It's a Deal

In the mid-twentieth century a definite camaraderie between American business and workers emerged, stemming from the unity that developed during and after World War II. In the 1950s and 60s, people made deals on a handshake. Integrity and honor toward your clients, customers, employers and employees seemed the order of the day. Workers could count on their loyalty being reciprocated with long-term employment, pensions and worker benefits. Lest we idealize this economic bliss, however, we must not forget its serious inconsistencies. Whole segments of the population like minorities and women were deliberately economically disenfranchised.

The Civil Rights Act of 1964 and the growing women's rights movement changed this environment by mandating that employers hire women and minorities. Even as the government stepped into the business arena and began regulating anti-social practices, these enforced economic changes met with fierce resistance. Society might have been changing but business was slowly following behind. Standing in 1960 and looking ahead forty-five years, would we ever have believed our economic and social structures would change as radically as they have? In today's world, for example, women are not only accepted in the workforce, but are huge contributors to it. Economic forces have changed so drastically in a few decades that staying at home as a mother or housewife is now a choice rather than a requirement. These economic and social changes occurred together.

Our society and our economic foundation have substantially progressed in the past couple of centuries, offering proof that we do change. Sometimes we change slowly and other times major technological advancements like the automobile or the Internet force us to change rapidly. Therefore instead of being pessimistic about the limitations of individuals and their profits, we should be optimistic and hopeful about a brighter future.

A New Mandate

There remain huge gaps in modern business that are ripe for transformation. The financial and corporate scandals of recent years reveal inequities that cry out for progress. These events reveal that dog-eat-dog capitalism still has a place in business. The father of laissez-faire capitalism, Adam Smith, declared that unfettered free markets best serve the public interest. He claimed an "invisible hand" (presumably God or Providence) guided all economic matters including individual greed. This "hand" was inherently just and fair, therefore human interference was unnecessary. As his nineteenth-century Scotland rebelled against Europe's imperial monopolies, Smith's concept of free enterprise was visionary. His economic treatise, *The Wealth of Nations*, was written while America was still a British colony. In the centuries since its publication, Adam Smith would surely have adapted his thesis to represent the vast changes in our modern world. Yet ironically, some twenty-first-century business thinkers continue to assert Smith's doctrine with very little variation. As recently as 1970, the renowned economist Milton Friedman claimed in a *New York Times* article, "The social responsibility of business is to increase profits." He explained that business has "no social conscience" and therefore no obligation to serve anything other than the economic bottom line. However, if we understand that the term *business* is synonymous with *people who produce, sell and buy*, then this statement reads, "People who produce, sell and buy have no social conscience." While this may often be true, it does not make it appropriate.

Friedman is not a capitalist without a conscience. He simply believes that business can inadvertantly do good works while focusing on profits. The fundamental problem of Friedman's declaration is that it ignores the big picture. This perspective does not include the role of business as it occurs in modern human existence. Inherent in this view is the definition of business as an inorganic entity detached from the human experience solely for the purpose of producing profit. This would be all well and good if business really was a soulless object with no connection to human experience.

However, what is business in reality? Business is the fruit of human effort. It is derived from groups of people in relationships with each other. We create business from human energy, utilizing the resources, ideas, efforts and cooperation of individuals. Clients and customers depend on our services or products to improve their lives. We in turn depend on their patronage to improve ours. Business is entirely dependent upon human beings for its sustainability. It is a reciprocal system of human effort for the benefit of human beings. Very simply, because business is a human activity, it has a fundamental social responsibility. Therefore if we reword Friedman's statement with this updated explanation of business it reads, "The economic responsibility of business is to maximize profits, while the social responsibility of business is to improve the lives of human beings."

THE SPIRITUAL LIFE OF BUSINESS

If the economic goal of business is to maximize profits, how can we also focus on improving people's lives? That is the dilemma for the modern enlightened business and the specific question addressed throughout the pages of *Spiritual Capitalism*. We are on the cusp of an evolution in business. It is one of the old versus the new, the traditional versus the cutting edge. Dog-eat-dog capitalism has no time for the ethical concerns of the masses. There is indeed no social conscience in its practice. Modern business as exemplified by growing movements like Corporate Social Responsibility is transforming rapidly. CSR describes the obligation corporations have to act in socially responsible ways in their communities and environment.

Groups like Spirit at Work, founded by Judi Neal, PhD, former management professor at the University of New Haven, actively inspire corporations and top management to include social progress in their bottom line. Other organizations like the World Business Academy include a network of powerful business leaders that encourage business to be "responsible in commerce, society and their own personal lives." Popular business commentators are addressing issues like outsourcing, corporate pay structure and acceptable profit margins on prime-time television. Former Federal Reserve Chairman Alan Greenspan publicly criticized corporate unethical behavior. Unquestionably a free market capitalist, there is a basic morality in Greenspan's message. The issues on the table are how much is enough when it comes to profit, and at what cost?

A shift has occurred in the way modern culture regards business after the scandals of the past few years. The long prison sentences given to corrupt corporate officers represent the current climate of social thought. The biggest change in our cultural views of business thievery since the 1980s is among business executives themselves. Twenty years ago while the general public vilified the greed of convicted Wall Street titans, the financial community revered them as mavericks. Recently a well-known financial journal quoted top CEOs who declared the twenty-five-year prison sentence received by Bernie Ebbers of WorldCom was appropriate while the four-year sentence of Dennis Kozlowski of Tyco was "too lenient." The mood in the business community is one of frustration and outrage at the criminal excesses of their colleagues. Business itself has become repulsed by this "take the money and run" thinking and a strong sense of ethical conduct has seeped into large portions of the world of finance.

Still, some old stalwart institutions and individuals ignore these movements and stick to their "profit at any cost" guns. Why shouldn't they defend their traditional practices? Business has been good to them. No one changes anything unless they are uncomfortable. Only when we are challenged at the deepest level can transformation take hold. The discontent of the general public with the status quo is threatening the comfort level of old-time capitalists.

The Gospel Truth

Thirty-five years ago, Milton Friedman's statement was accepted as gospel truth. However in the first decade of the twenty-first century, this sentiment seems grossly inadequate by many profit-minded entrepreneurs. More appropriate for modernity is the need to redefine business as having "the social responsibility to increase profits *while benefiting humanity.*" This is the challenge we are charged with as members of an enlightened society. We know we can maximize "profits at any cost." Making money without giving thought to others or the community at large has been done for millennia. It requires little of our minds and hearts to do so. The task for modern-thinking persons is to use our resources in our work and business, to create profit and simultaneously create a better world for ourselves and posterity. A tall order perhaps, but in the pages that follow you will find examples of hugely successful individuals who have done just that. We depict billionaires and corporate officers who have created fortunes and improved the lives of all those they touched. If they can do it, so can we.

Spiritual Capitalism provides a road map of how you can pursue profit and still benefit humanity through socially responsible means. It takes the concepts of CSR one step further, making them personal. While corporate and government entities have their duty to honor their constituents, so do we individually. The purpose of this book is to shine a light on that individual responsibility and detail a practical guide for its implementation.

Wall Street as a Role Model

Finally as we suspend our doubts over the moral advancement of humankind, remarks that members of the media made in the past year come to mind. "Is Wall Street as corrupt as it seems?" asked one mid-western talk show host. Or more to the point as a South Florida radio host queried, "Are they really all crooks on Wall Street?" We hadn't thought much about this before. We pondered these questions and reviewed the past years as partners in our highly competitive field of Wall Street headhunting. We remembered countless business transactions with corporate managers, investment bankers, Wall Street traders and salespersons. These included deals with some of the most influential market makers at the most powerful investment banks in the world. When we did the numbers, we were shocked by what we discovered. Thinking back over a very profitable decade, we could only remember a handful of individuals out of thousands of associates that actually tried to cheat us. Of the many money managers, bankers, masters of the universe and financial wizards we dealt with only a small percentage (perhaps 20%-30%) had been dishonest. The rest, the vast majority of Wall Street businesspeople that we worked with, had given us their word as their bond, honored deals with a handshake and stood by their principles. An astounding 70% of our Wall Street colleagues conducted their business with integrity.

We realized we have met far more people of honor than not, giving us hope for the message herein. If this is true on Wall Street, we can only suppose it to be true throughout the rest of the business world.

The Change is in the Air

In the following pages we detail our personal and professional experiences through one of the pivotal events of the modern century and use it as a metaphor for social change. Traumatic events in our lives can help us transform to higher levels of thought. We can learn important lessons through our suffering and move to the next level of our social economic evolution. There is a natural progression in our thinking—an intellectual awareness that takes place first inside of ourselves and then spills out into the world. It moves us to merge our personal value system with our common economic practices.

The joint effort of the world's richest businessmen, Bill Gates and Warren Buffett, to give their billions "back to society," signals an extraordinary shift in modern capitalism. It is no longer acceptable to serve only yourself without thought to others. The change is in the air. We feel the change when we visit college campuses or when we travel the country to speak to corporate and community groups. Their enthusiasm inspires us to continue. We experience it when we participate in the many conferences for enlightened business.

Spiritual Capitalism may not answer all your questions, but it will resolve many of them. The rest is up to you individually to discover how to include a practice of spiritual capitalism in your everyday pursuit of profit. Frankly, it's just good business.

◆

Chapter 1

What the Fire Department of New York

Taught Wall Street About Money

*"Firefighters are the purest
example of love that
we have in our society."*

RUDY GIULIANI
NEW YORK CITY MAYOR

*C*hapter 1

What the Fire Department of New York

Taught Wall Street About Money

THE whole world changed for us on September 11, 2001. For twenty-one years before that, Peter had been working relatively peacefully on Wall Street, and the last eleven of those years we worked together. We broke off from a larger firm in the mid-1990s and opened our own executive search firm, specializing in institutional debt and equity, sales and trading. In layman's terms, this translates to headhunters for the bond and equity markets. For example, if an investment bank needs to find a new head for its corporate bond desk, we look for someone to fill the position who is currently employed at another firm. In a sense, what we do is a type of high-finance espionage. Our main clients retain our services and include the top investment banking firms, commercial banks and hedge funds.

The companies we work for, in our opinion, are the best money firms in the industry—not because they employ us, but because we would not represent them if this weren't true. We stand behind all of our client companies—part of our successful sales pitch is that these firms are worthy of the people they employ. They are team players. They treat people right. They operate at the highest level of business conduct. We cannot sell the firm unless we believe this.

We deal with some of most brilliant minds in business today. These are market movers and individuals who shape the industry. They often change firms for a variety of reasons. Sometimes it is for more money, but not always. Frequently individuals change firms for personal reasons—better cultural fit, location, or work environment, more upside and advancement. We are successful only when we find someone who is not satisfied in their current position. When an individual leaves a firm, opportunity arises for others to fill their shoes. Wall Street thrives on continual motion and change. One thing you can be sure of is that nothing will remain the same for very long.

As time passed, we hired more people and expanded our business into two areas. The first was generating income through Wall Street search. The second was investing that income in real estate development. We would take the profits from Wall Street and buy commercial and residential properties in New York City, the Hamptons and other waterfront communities on Long Island. We had been lucky enough along the way to develop a friend, Mark, who was a seasoned veteran of the Fire Department of the City of New York and a building contractor as well—a one-man dynamo. When we were considering a real estate investment, Mark would discuss the reconstruction possibilities with us before any contract was signed. Upon his structural approval, we would purchase the property. Then we designed and supervised the renovation together. Mark would act as foreman and contract out the specialty work to other firefighters. Some of the firefighters were active members of the FDNY. Others were volunteer or retired firemen with contracting businesses. (New York City firefighters generally work two days on and two days off. They are paid between $26,000 and $58,000 a year. A modest home in the New York metropolitan area costs around $500,000. This reality often forces New York City firefighters to take second jobs in order to support their families in one of the most expensive cities in the world.)

Whether volunteer, active or retired, they had the same work ethic. The firefighters immediately formed a cohesive team. No one competed with anyone else. There was immediate respect between them. The goal of the firefighters was to get the job done as quickly and efficiently as possible. There wasn't anything they couldn't do and do well. From working with these firemen we realized that firefighters don't know how to say, "No, I can't do it." They only think, "We'll figure it out." Nothing was ever sloppy or half-finished. They were perfectionists.

The first property we renovated with Mark and our firefighter crew was a residential property in East Hampton. What normally would have taken six months to complete took these men two and a half. At any moment, the house was filled with four to eight firefighters. When they needed to leave, replacements took over. Having been used to a firehouse schedule, they used the same work pattern with us. They worked for 16 hours, slept for 4 hours, woke up and worked again. Mark had things organized like a firehouse. Everyone knew their job and executed it. These were the hardest working people we had ever met. There were none of the usual problems that can occur in construction, where the job takes twice as long or the workers don't show up. These men moved into the empty house and basically camped out for two months. The workforce we developed with Mark's assistance was extraordinary. We had never seen anything like it before, except on Wall Street.

Successful Wall Streeters eat, drink and sleep their business. They work twenty-four hours a day, seven days a week. This is how you make money and keep your edge. We often received e-mails on a weeknight written at 1:30 in the morning from clients who finally had time to reply. For years, we ran our business this way, and through this level of commitment, we developed and expanded quickly.

A New World

But for us, all that changed on September 11. As the Twin Towers fell on that tragic day, our two worlds, Wall Street and the Fire Department of the City of New York, collided. As members of the Wall Street community with close connections to many local firefighters, we were immediately plunged into a life-and-death struggle of mammoth proportions. Father Mychal Judge, the New York City Fire Department chaplain and personal friend, was the first official casualty of the attack on the World Trade Center. The death of Father Mike, a wise and gentle Franciscan priest, was a jarring reality for us. His passing represented the loss of innocence in the face of this absolute cruelty. Our business screeched to an abrupt halt as our personal lives filled with anguish.

On September 11, all of us on Wall Street, in the New York City Fire Department and all the other victims of the catastrophe became one. Politicians, the medical community, iron, steel, construction and sanitation workers worked day and night with the EMS, police and fire departments in the rescue and recovery efforts. Suddenly, we had the unique vantage point of seeing the tragedy from both sides: the rescued and the rescuers, the money-obsessed world of Wall Street and the life-saving world of the New York City Fire Department. As the months passed, we heard daily reports from colleagues and friends in the financial industry of their miraculous escapes, as well as the latest counts of those missing. Simultaneously, our firemen friends came to our home after a tour at Ground Zero and filled us in on the horrors of their digging. We listened to the heartache of the firemen who attended no less than 47 funerals in two months. Their anguish was matched by their

Wall Street counterparts. An investment banker colleague of ours said, "I lost 27 people in the Towers. I don't know what to think anymore."

Miraculously, Mark and all of our firefighting crew made it through that day. My brother, who worked near One World Trade Center, and many of our closest associates in the financial community made it through too. But each of us had a tragic tale to tell. We all lost friends and loved ones along with our innocence that day. In the months to come, Wall Street put its faith and trust in the fire department. The entire Wall Street community held the New York City Fire Department and all the other uniformed service personnel in reverence. We were awed by their extraordinary bravery in the face of such shocking brutality. Their suffering mirrored ours. They were everyone's inspiration to go on, to contribute in whatever way we could. For all of us in the financial community, it was hard to believe in our work anymore.

For the first time ever, Wall Street stopped and questioned itself. "Was it all worth it?" we asked. In the words of one investment banker, "Next to the rescue workers, nothing we do seems important." For an unprecedented moment in history, Wall Street took its eyes off money. Instead, life and love became our priority. Many of us on Wall Street forgot about ourselves. We didn't think about the deals, the markets, the trades or outdoing each other. We thought only about reaching out and helping the person next to us. Wall Street had always been about money. For us personally, it was a privilege to be part of the community and to have that opportunity. Only now this seemed frivolous. Watching people jump out of buildings, knowing some of them were our friends was hard to forget. Their senseless agony and loss made everything else seem futile.

For the next year, it was tough to find passion for our ordinary jobs. Making money lost its appeal. Many of us on Wall Street thought maybe it was too much of a sacrifice.

We questioned our vocation and thought of getting out. *It isn't supposed to be like this.* Some, who could afford to, quit. Others stayed in. For the sake of our colleagues, our city and our country, we had to push on and rebuild the economy. It was our duty.

For the first time ever, the Fire Department of the City of New York stopped and questioned itself. "Was it all worth it?" they asked. Firefighting had never been about money. For them, preserving life had always been the priority. Only now they weren't fighting fires. They were cleaning up the battle-field of an unprovoked war. A member of Engine 14 echoed the thoughts of many: "This isn't what we signed on for."

Firefighters are a select group. For some it is an inherited privilege, the skills handed down over generations. Others, who yearn to be part of this great tradition, work hard to pass the tests and get in. It is an honor to be chosen, a privilege to be among them. Now, watching their brethren fall to their doom and terror grip the streets, they thought maybe it was too much of a sacrifice. They questioned their vocation and thought of getting out. *It isn't supposed to be like this.* For the sake of their brothers, their city, their country, they stayed in and searched among the ruins for nothing but peace. They had to push on and rebuild the city. It was their duty.

What became crystal clear to us in that year as we confronted so much suffering, was that all we really had in the end was each other. In those days, weeks and months, the kindness and caring of others to us and us to them gave meaning to our existence. A multimillionaire financial advisor sat down with the widows of the Windows on the World waiters and busboys, mostly minimum-wage earners with no insurance, and asked, "How can I help you manage through the coming months?" People of all economic backgrounds volunteered every resource they had to help ease the suffering of others. Our hearts were broken for those faces of the missing plastered on every available wall, unwittingly creating a memorial to the dead. There were so many offers for volunteers by New Yorkers and the nation alike that the mayor had to turn people away. It was America's worst moment and America's shining moment all at once. People by the millions were so moved by the suffering of strangers that for a brief moment in time, they put aside their own needs and thought only about others. Surely in this we saw grace.

Many people were asking where in all this horror was God. But our faith in a greater purpose to our lives carried us through these painful days. We hoped eventually to find some meaning in this, some positive lessons to be learned.

Business as Usual

In the immediate aftermath, the love and support that New Yorkers received from all over the country and the world was gratifying. We felt the genuine concern of people everywhere. It uplifted us in our sorrow. Then, slowly, people resumed their lives. Even New Yorkers who were removed from Wall Street, downtown New York and the task of rebuilding Ground Zero lost their focus on the tragedy. After just three months, it became time to move on. Suddenly, it was "business as usual" again.

For those of us who had our lives and businesses paralyzed by the attack, this wasn't easy to do. Over the next year, we lost 90% of our income and business, but still considered ourselves lucky. We had been much more fortunate than many others we knew. We were alive, so were our families and most of our friends. Our survival was priceless.

In the next few months, we went through the motions of business. It seemed empty to us now. We watched as the landscape of our city and our work was irrevocably changed. We stood by, feeling helpless, as our city's bravest rebuilt our world. How could we go back to business as usual? This was just not possible anymore.

The Sins of the City

There were some who thought this tremendous tragedy was God's justice, punishment for the Wall Street wicked. A small percentage of people viewed our city as a modern-day Sodom and Gomorrah, and decided we got what we deserved. Yet no one looking around at New York that day would claim our suffering was justified. The faces of anguished firefighters reflected the despair in us all.

New York includes everything human, good and bad. Every state in the country, every country and culture in the world is represented, and that's what makes it such a great experiment. The success of our coexistence in New York offers possibilities for the rest of the world.

However, the great majority of the free world did feel our sorrow and suffered with us. Together, we formed a loud and unified voice and agreed we would not stand idly by and let hatred triumph over goodness. It woke us out of our sleepy comfort and electrified us as a people. We heard the courageous last words of the victims on their deadly flights and the heart-wrenching voice mail messages of those who fell with the Towers. We saw the frightened eyes of Father Mike, captured on video as he stood in the lobby of One World Trade Center. The outpouring of love was phenomenal. It took this monumental tragedy for us to see the inherent goodness in people everywhere. It would be our challenge, as a people, not to forget what we learned in those moments about the possibilities for the future, where the concerns of the individual alone are not the only things that matter.

THE HARSH REALITY OF MONEY

As partners, Peter and I had to put our business back together as quickly as possible. We needed to make money, even if it seemed insignificant to us now. This was a cold, harsh reality. We owed it to our children, our staff, our community and ourselves. In those first few months, we resisted an overwhelming urge to move to New England and put our heads in the sand. "Anywhere but here," we thought. "This is just too ugly to bear." We dreamed of a simpler life: an eight-hour workday, time to rest, relax, read and write. But our friends and our city needed us. We could not walk out on them. We asked Firefighter Mark, now a rescue worker at Ground Zero, what we could do to help. He said, "Go hug your children. You never know how much time you have left."

We began changing our work patterns. In all the years we had been in business together, we waited for the day we could take time off. We thought someday, when the kids were older, we'd relax. All of a sudden, we realized we couldn't wait. The time to do the things we wanted to do was now. We began sharing the driving of our six-year-old to school. We reclaimed Sunday as our day of rest. We no longer put off visiting relatives and friends—we had more patience for their idiosyncrasies and our own. In the next year, from our tremendous sadness, there emerged a deeper level of living.

THE BRAVE FACE OF LOVE

The dedication and commitment of the FDNY to the city of New York remained our daily inspiration. The firefighters were the very definition of courage. Each day they put aside their grief to search through the rubble in order to lessen the hurt of the living. At Ground Zero, a rescue worker was looking through binoculars at a pile of debris seven stories high.

He pointed to the pile and said, "Eighteen of my friends are in there." The enormity of his suffering was beyond comprehension. We worried about the degree of stress the digging efforts were putting on our firefighter friends. We asked Mark why he had to be there. "I want to be there," he said. "I requested it."

What the world may not have realized was that our Wall Street community was doing the same. Inspired by our firefighter colleagues, Wall Street put on a brave face. While still mourning themselves, many Wall Streeters marched to work each day through the hideous smell of rotting flesh. All of us worked to put the pieces of the puzzle back together.

While the Wall Street community felt grateful for the rescue workers surrounding us, we realized something remarkable. These firefighters were doing the impossible, methodically digging through the wreckage every day searching for the remains of loved ones to give closure to themselves and the families of those lost. Suddenly Peter and I understood: it was all about *love*. Everything firefighters did was for love: the love of their colleagues, their families, their friends, their community, their country. The entire financial community realized that the brave FDNY was the very face of love. On that tragic day and in the months that followed, Wall Street learned the meaning of love from the Fire Department of New York.

Witnessing these selfless actions changed the way Peter and I thought about our own work. Like the firefighters, we saw that everything we did was for love. Our business endeavors were no exception. We worked to create a good life for our loved ones because without them in our lives, no amount of profit made any difference. After this realization, it was not possible for us to go back to simply making money. If we were to continue in business, we must combine making money with a deeper spiritual purpose, a more spiritual capitalism. We had to find a way to replace the survival-of-the-fittest philosophy we were used to with a more inclusive and thoughtful ideology.

For years, we had run our business with integrity. Yet we always viewed our spiritual life and our economic endeavors as two separate realities. Now we saw them as the same. We understood that the freedom to pursue wealth was a basic capitalistic ideal. However, after witnessing the work of the firefighters, we also understood that wealth gained without thought to others was no gain at all. In order to give our work a deeper meaning, we must incorporate our social conscience into our material pursuits. From this day on, we could only proceed in business as *spiritual* capitalists by consciously combining the pursuit of profit with caring for the world around us.

Lesson 1

Business is personal

*"I was a human being before
I became a businessman."*

GEORGE SOROS
BILLIONAIRE, CEO

Lesson 1

Business is personal

IN modern business, people have been operating under the common misconception that the pursuit of money is not personal, though everything you do in any area of your life is personal. Whether at home, at play or at work, your actions affect whomever you come in contact with. What you do privately for your family and friends and publicly for acquaintances and strangers is equally personal for you and for them. You are what you do, all that you do, including what you do for a living.

Love doesn't mean much to us when we think of business. The word love has many different meanings. In your family, love might mean loyalty, support and commitment to the welfare of one another. In the bigger picture of the world, it means empathy for each other through our shared human experience. Each of us needs to broaden our understanding of love or empathy to include the experiences of people we know very little or not at all. You have a responsibility first to yourself, then to your dependents or loved ones and finally to the greater world you live in.

When we think of our families and our friends we easily see our actions towards them as personal. Yet when we venture beyond our inner circle to the larger arena at work, somehow we throw all we know out the window. They are not our family or friends; therefore what we do to them is not personal. What if our firefighters were to say that, or our nurses, doctors or caregivers? "You are not my friend or my family; therefore what I do to you is not personal. Your welfare is of no concern to me." Wouldn't we be outraged? Yet no firefighter would ever say this. Through the course of their work, firefighters believe the life and welfare of every stranger is as personal to them as their own.

Why as business owners, workers, employers or employees do we feel our indifference to others is appropriate? How do we separate ourselves so completely from others when it comes to money? In our private lives, if a spouse betrayed their partner, could he (or she) excuse his actions by claiming the infidelity was not personal? How then do we justify this in our business affairs? When you convince yourself that your business endeavors are separate from you, you are really saying, "I do not want to answer for my own actions." The myth of business as "nothing personal" is an example of the power of denial. If it derives from human energy and affects human lives, what could be more personal? Profit, we have assured ourselves, is something inanimate not human-made. Therefore, we don't have to answer personally for our actions. Basic business teaching claims our sole focus is profit without side issues like responsibility to anyone other than shareholders. However, don't shareholders have a responsibility also for how their investments affect others?

What about our duty to our employees, employers, suppliers, consumers, and the communities we operate in? Profit is money in our pocket. Yet whose lives were disrupted to put it there? Who do I affect personally by what I do? Do I add value to their lives or take value away? Can I maximize my profits, keep my competitive edge and still concern myself with the effect my actions are having on others, seen and unseen?

The claim that what we do in business is not personal is a deliberate deception. Business understands its personal connection with us; otherwise it would not market itself that way. Advertisers pitch products and services to our personal needs. They want us to believe a company is concerned about us. They emphasize cultural values. We are told a product brings our family closer, makes us happier or more secure. One company calls itself, "A good neighbor that cares." Another states, "For us, its personal." These claims offer clear evidence that business grasps its personal nature. Yet if we really examined their actions would we still think they care?

Over time we have accepted the fallacy of business as impersonal and called it truth. We have nurtured this concept, given it life and substance. We believe it simply because we have repeated it over and over. Yet there is a huge chasm between what we wish to believe and what actually occurs.

The monumental market scandals over the past few years bring to the surface the need for our business practices to evolve. As we look back we see the personal consequences for millions of people from these fiascoes—the bankruptcies, lawsuits, fortunes lost, retirements interrupted and futures irrevocably changed. Clearly if it is business, it is personal to someone.

In the survival-of-the-fittest capitalistic thinking, personal accountability does not figure in our business or monetary pursuits. Just as we have progressed in our conscious thought about other social issues in the last century, it is time for us to shed this limiting belief about the pursuit of profit. The next step in our money evolution is to change our philosophy from survival-of-the-fittest to a more appropriate responsibility-of-the-fittest. The strongest among us, especially those with the means, position and influence should remember our responsibility to others while in the pursuit of material success.

> ### KEY POINTS IN LESSON ONE
>
> › Everything you do in business is personal to someone.
>
> › The claim that business is not personal is a deliberate deception.
>
> › *Responsibility-of-the-fittest* must replace *survival-of-the-fittest*.

HOW DOES LESSON ONE MANIFEST IN YOUR BUSINESS LIFE?

EXAMPLE #1

CHIEF OPERATING OFFICER, *WALL STREET INVESTMENT BANK*

Three boys grew up as best friends in a small New Jersey town. Each dreamed of making it big. They promised each other that whoever made it first would help the others on their way. The three ended up working on Wall Street at the same investment bank. As they climbed their way up the corporate ladder, the easy dynamic they enjoyed as children began to change for one of the three. As his comrades rose through the ranks quickly, feelings of jealousy and competition began to bubble up inside of him. His boyhood friends were appointed president of the investment bank and head of fixed income global trading, respectively. Rather than feeling joy at their success, he felt a burning desire to unseat them. As head of fixed income sales, he enjoyed great status and wealth. But a part of him wanted to be more important than his friends. When the friend who was president began to experience difficulties in his personal life, this man saw his opportunity. He maneuvered a coup to push him out of the firm and quickly rose to the position himself.

When he finally gained the power he strove for, all the years of callous actions caught up with him. He was feared and hated by his employees. Colleagues knew he could not be trusted or taken at his word. His personal life suffered greatly. As a result of his deception, he lost both boyhood friends. Shortly thereafter, his wife sued for divorce and an ugly custody battle over their two children followed. She received full custody of their children and a large portion of his wealth. In his lack of concern for others, he achieved great wealth, power and status. Yet he lost everyone he loved. In the end, he had all the outer trappings of great success, but none of the personal support that a different approach might have yielded.

EXAMPLE #2

HEAD OF GLOBAL FIXED INCOME, WALL STREET INVESTMENT BANK

A young man joined a Wall Street firm fresh with the enthusiasm of a sharp and creative mind. He was extraordinarily resourceful and brilliant. He created new ways to make money that made many people very rich, which also made him very rich. By his early thirties, he was in a top management position at a prestigious investment bank, and a superstar on Wall Street. He became one of the most influential persons in the investment banking world. He created whole new industries with his monetary inventions. On his quick climb up, he brought along friends and associates that he respected and loved. He shared his success with whomever he could. If he met someone that showed ability and integrity, he tried to find a place for him or her at his firm. He surrounded himself with people like him, loyal and ethical. In the world of cutthroat business deal-

ings, he was a man of his word. If he made a commitment, he kept his promise, even if market conditions changed.

Unexpectedly, at the age of fifty, he died of a brain aneurysm. His entire firm was devastated and anguished over his loss. At his funeral, more than a thousand people attended and mourned his passing. From janitors to senators, people spoke of him with love and admiration, expressing how this man had touched their lives in a profound way. He was described as generous and kind, a great father, husband, son, friend, colleague and employer. He would be missed by so many.

This remarkable man lived his life to the fullest. He achieved extraordinary success and tremendous wealth at a young age. Yet he never forgot about others along the way, because he truly understood that business was personal. His concern for others profoundly changed the course of hundreds of people's lives who were lucky enough to know him.

APPLYING LESSON ONE TO YOUR LIFE

At the end of your life, you are measured by and measure yourself by what and who you are to others. Money and the accumulation of wealth are secondary to our relationships. Will you be remembered as a good father or mother, a good wife or husband, a good son or daughter, a good friend or colleague? As the true story above reveals, it is possible to pursue profit and achieve great financial success and still remain considerate of others. Anyone who has achieved material success without spiritual success knows this is a hollow victory. It is a clear choice. At any given point, you can decide to include concern for others in your pursuit of profit.

Tools to Include Spiritual Success in Your Material Success

> Make your relationship with loved ones more important than your relationship with money.

> Be aware of how your business actions affect everyone involved personally.

> Take responsibility for your actions in the pursuit of profit.

Creating a New vision of Business as Personal

Remember how important people are to your happiness. Include consideration for others in your pursuit of money and all that you do. Examine your work and business activities and recognize how they affect others. Accept that there are times when you must make difficult and unpopular decisions. Have the courage to make those choices after you consider all possibilities and are ready to take responsibility for them. Remember that what makes a life well lived are your actions along the way that make a positive difference in other people's lives.

Chapter 2

Money: The Root of All Evil?

"*If only there were evil people somewhere insidiously committing evil deeds, and it were necessary only to separate them from the rest of us and destroy them. But the line dividing good and evil cuts through the heart of every human being.*"

ALEXANDER SOLZHENITSYN
AUTHOR, SOVIET DISSIDENT

Money: The Root of All Evil?

IMMEDIATELY after the tragedy, both of our businesses were in limbo. The Wall Street deals we had on the table before 9/11 were postponed indefinitely. Every search we had on September 10 was cancelled the following week. Our real estate projects were put on hold, as our firemen crew became rescue workers at Ground Zero. This new reality occurred overnight. In the next year, the entire nature of our business changed. For many of us in New York that day, life as we knew it was over.

In the months that followed, money became an important issue for everyone involved. The U.S. economy was threatened, and the city's economy was devastated. Having lost their wage earners, many of the victims' families struggled financially. In addition, thousands of survivors, like restaurant workers, secretaries, security personnel, small business people, computer programmers and many other workers lost their jobs and wondered how to make ends meet. Unemployment in the city swelled to monumental proportions. According to an article in a well-respected business journal, more than 75,000 people in New York City lost their jobs in the first month alone. Hundreds of businesses disappeared overnight and many more went bankrupt in the year after the attack. The owners of mom-and-pop businesses like souvenir shops and newspaper stores who lost everything stood in long lines at Pier 94, hoping for money to pay their electric bills. Money became a major issue for all of us who remained alive.

September 11 reminded us that next to life itself, nothing else was important. The individuals who faced the last moments of their lives were not thinking about money; they were thinking of love. In those first days and weeks after the attack this is all any of us thought about.

As the dust settled and we began to come to grips with our losses, the overriding issue for many of us emerged: money. We needed money to live. All of us had bills to pay. Despite our grief, each of us, the fire department, the police department, the financial community, workers of all kinds, needed to earn a living. Wall Street had an economy to repair. New York had a city to rebuild. This reality did not disappear just because we were faced with death. For survivors, like everyone else in our capitalistic world, money was crucial for our existence. As time wore on, the victims' families became more and more vocal about demanding compensation for their losses. Some critics viewed it as greed. We all wondered how we could put a dollar amount on life and love. Yet the unrelenting reality was that the living needed money to live. They could not be compensated for their lost love. Yet, as a matter of necessity, they must be compensated for their loved ones' lost earnings.

In the glare of the tragedy, life, love and money were completely entwined. It was easy to see that love was connected to our spiritual selves, but what about money? How could something this essential to our existence be disconnected from our true core? When faced with life and death where all trivial issues are put aside, little else matters but love. Yet when the reality of living surfaces again, in practical terms, little matters more than money. Therefore, even though money is clearly not a thing to replace human substance, neither is it a thing to be ignored.

It's Only Money

We have often been taught that money is the root of all evil. This view portrays money as a sinister force with the power to corrupt us. Yet we are also taught to make as much money as possible. This contradiction confuses us. When we questioned the motives of the 9/11 victims' families who asked for compensation, some of us thought, "It's about money, isn't it?" Yes, it is about money—for all of us. In our world, money is vital to life itself, but it doesn't have to be evil. If we believe it is, we must surely see in it a reflection of ourselves. Money wasn't evil when the nation expressed its love by contributing to the victims' funds. It wasn't evil when the firefighters had to go back to their jobs to pay the bills. Nor was it evil when the thousands of unemployed had to apply for unemployment compensation.

At what point do we decide whether money is worthy of our devotion or contempt? Money has the power to corrupt us only if we use it that way. It is evil when it motivates us to cause suffering to others. But then it is really us who possess the evil, not money itself. Surely with or without money, there would be evil in the world. There would still be hate, depravity, domination, slaughter, torture and every other imaginable form of intentional cruelty that exists, because human nature, not money, is the driving force behind it.

Many of us hold a fundamental belief that money makes otherwise good people do bad things. A dear friend of ours, a self-made businesswoman, recently asked us, "Why do you think money corrupts people?" We responded that we didn't think money corrupted anyone. People were corrupted by their own thoughts, not money. Our evidence for this belief stemmed from the fact that we knew many people of means who were honorable in every way. Conversely, we knew other individuals of little or no means who were corrupt in many ways.

Money has the ability to test us. It tests our faith, our fear and our loyalty. It reveals our selfishness, compassion, ego, generosity, creativity, our sense of responsibility and ability to love. Through our relationship with money, our real selves are challenged and exposed. If money in our life makes us do evil or harmful things to others, it is only because that aspect of our personality was already there. Our desire for money gives us the opportunity to act as our best or worst selves.

Blood Money

What our attackers understood on that September morning was that our survival and future depended on money. Therefore, killing us and taking our lives was not enough. They must also attack and destroy our ability to create money. That was the message. Kill as many people as possible, and then kill the money machine behind them. Without money, they hoped the great Goliath would lose its strength. So they targeted one of the greatest visible symbols of capitalism in our culture, the Twin Towers of the World Trade Center. These murderers could not have expected to destroy as much as they did. Yet they must have understood the symbolism: *We are killing you and your money.*

And so they did. As our business crumbled and came to a standstill for the next year, we began to realize how truly successful they were. While New Yorkers suffered personal losses of life and limb, we also struggled to survive financially. In all our years in this country of privilege, we never fully understood until that moment how absolutely dependent our lives had been upon money. We were used to our abundance. We took for granted having more food than we could eat, more blessings than we could count. We took for granted that the Towers themselves would always be there.

It became unmistakably clear: our blood, love and our money were our lifeline. We could not disregard our need for money any more than we could ignore the meaning of love in our lives. After the tragedy, we were reminded that life itself was most precious, and that love was most important to our hearts. Yet we also recognized that after life and love, money was an essential ingredient to continuing our lives. Therefore, money was not a wicked by-product of the human mind, some necessary evil separate from us. Something this important to our lives did not exist by chance but by higher purpose. Each of us could choose to use money to harm others or help them. By doing good, we could use our pursuit of money to advance our spiritual growth—rather than limit it.

◆

Lesson 2

Use your pursuit of money as a tool for good

"Money is only a tool. It will take you wherever you wish, but it will not replace you as the driver."

AYN RAND
WRITER, PHILOSOPHER

Lesson 2

Use your pursuit of money as a tool for good

WHAT exactly is money? Money is the product of our energy and ingenuity. The exchange of money is a form of barter created for the divine purpose of continuing and maintaining human life. When we exchange money for goods or services we create a sacred covenant with each other. We buy things that sustain or comfort us. In return we give money earned from our labor. How did this spiritual exchange become a tool for evil in many of our minds?

When we perceive the inanimate object of money as corrupting we confirm the illogical beliefs we carry within ourselves. If money is evil, then we ourselves are not responsible. We rationalize our poverty as something noble. Or we believe our wealth is the result of divine approval. Money has no power without us who use it. We direct its intent and value in our lives.

The concept of good and evil isn't as simple as the good guys and bad guys. Within all of us is both good and bad. We have good thoughts and sometimes what could be described as evil thoughts. We have good behavior and at times we do things that even we know we shouldn't. Self-righteousness aside, no human being is exempt from this reality. Before we can eradicate evil in others, we need to eliminate it in ourselves. This includes our thoughts and actions around money. If we use our pursuit and accumulation of money as a positive force in the world, we uplift ourselves. However, if we use money to diminish others, we diminish our spiritual selves in the process.

Possessions do not create evil in us. Lack of compassion and consideration for others creates our spiritual illness. Evil is a cancer of the mind, and spreads rapidly through our spirit. If our thoughts are hateful, miserly and indifferent, so will our lives be. If our thoughts are compassionate and concerned, our lives take on deeper meaning.

We are born unequally in many ways, with different opportunities and challenges, including our ethical foundations. Some of us are fortunate to inherit good ethics from our parents. Others learn unethical behavior early in life. Although we enter this world with differing paths, we are assured of equal opportunity in one area: the freedom to choose. Every one of us has the power to choose how we will act within our particular set of circumstances. The spiritual quality of "free will" enables us individually and independently of others to choose good or evil. As we look back through history, many "good" people did "bad" things. Sometimes they were well intentioned but acted unreasonably. Sometimes they rationalized their destructive behavior and claimed it was for the common good.

As we progress as a species, our concept of what is good and evil also evolves. There have been dramatic changes in our thinking of what is acceptable behavior and what is not. Less than two centuries ago in America, a "good person" could beat his wife, abuse his children, bribe lawmakers and own slaves with society's approval. In our modern view, honoring life is good behavior. Damaging the quality of life of others through the pursuit of money at any cost falls under the heading of evil.

Understanding this is the first step to your money enlightenment. How you use money determines its spiritual purpose in your life. Viewing money as the root of all evil allows you to believe money itself dictates your actions. Money is not a thing that controls you. You control it.

Evil is potentially within all of us, and so is good. Therefore, we must decide within the deepest parts of our souls, individually and then collectively, how to use money for the purpose of good. What is *good*? Simply put, good is that which enhances rather than destroys.

KEY POINTS IN LESSON TWO

› When we exchange money for goods or services we create a sacred covenant with each other.

› Money is not a thing that controls you—you control it.

› *Good* is that which enhances, *evil* is that which destroys.

HOW DOES LESSON TWO MANIFEST IN YOUR MONEY LIFE?

EXAMPLE #1

INDEPENDENT THEATRICAL PRODUCER

A theatrical producer in New York saved a great deal of money in his early years by selling illegal drugs. He rationalized to himself that he needed seed money to get ahead. As he accumulated enough funds to invest in other things, he began earning a living legitimately. By age thirty-five, he was earning what most people considered an enormous sum. He enjoyed bragging about his fortune to the struggling actors around him. He would flash ten-thousand-dollar packs of hundred-dollar-bills in front of the impoverished performers and laugh. He used his wealth to manipulate a coterie of hangers-on by offering them just enough financial help to be dependent on him, but never free of him. Their devotion assured him that he would never be lonely. Somewhere underneath that deceptive exterior, he had a good heart, but he rarely let anyone see it. He thought people were not to be trusted, that they just use you, so you should use them first.

When this man lay dying of cancer at the age of forty-eight, he found himself virtually alone. Most of his wealth had been spent on medical bills. His hangers-on had no more interest in him. He had chased away anyone that truly cared for him years before, with his cynicism and cruelty. His use of money as a tool to control others severely inhibited any spiritual growth he might otherwise have found.

EXAMPLE #2

CHIEF FINANCIAL OFFICER, BROADWAY COSTUME DESIGN COMPANY

There wasn't anyone close to this man who didn't absolutely adore him. In every area of his life, he shared his success with others. At his day job as a corporate officer for a prestigious Broadway costume design company, colleagues learned to depend on his creative brilliance, generosity and humor. He pulled the company out of financial straits to top-notch success and gave the credit to his staff. When he left the company due to terminal illness, he insisted that his assistant take over his coveted job.

In the evenings, he was the beloved manager for a world-renowned jazz musician. This arrangement came about when he heard of the musician's unjust record company deal, and he offered to negotiate. They became best friends as well as business associates.

He also supported a talented yet unknown painter, whose work he discovered years ago, by guiding him on marketing strategies. He raved about the artist's work to every art enthusiast he met, bought many of his paintings and helped him arrange gallery showings around town. He thought it was a shame that the artist had never been to Paris, so he surprised him with a ten-day, all-expenses-paid trip, complete with museum guides and restaurant recommendations. In his last days in the hospital, he was surrounded by a roomful of family and friends. A year later, more than a hundred people crammed a well-known jazz club in Greenwich Village for an evening of loving tribute to him. He had spent the greater portion of his life helping others learn what was easy for him: how to attain material success while using it as a tool for spiritual growth.

Applying Lesson Two to Your Life

Sometimes we live life as if we can go on forever. We might convince ourselves we never have to answer for anything we do along the way. Then a tragedy like September 11 or the loss of a loved one reminds us of the fragility and brevity of human life. All of us will have to answer eventually, if not to God, then at least to ourselves. In death, we face a universal truth—we die as we lived. If we live in love, we end our lives that way. If we live in bitterness, so it is with our final moments. We need other people who care about us in our lives. This is what makes life worth living, seeing the reflection of love or regard in another person's eyes.

Tools to Help You Control Your Use of Money

› Use your pursuit of money as a tool for good.

› Recognize that your money behavior is within your control.

› Use money to expand your personal growth, not diminish it.

Creating a Vision for Using Money to Generate Good in Your Life

Choose to use your pursuit of money for the purpose of good, not evil. Use the pursuit of material success to expand your spiritual growth by enhancing the quality of life for everyone around you. Remember that you have the power to use money as a tool for a deeper self-awareness. Examine what your money behavior reveals about your character and make the necessary changes to use money as a tool for good.

◆

Chapter 3

An American Tragedy

> *"He that is of the opinion money will do everything may well be suspected of doing everything for money."*
>
> BEN FRANKLIN
> FOUNDING FATHER

An American Tragedy

FROM September 10 to September 12, the difference in our local economy was extraordinary. During the remarkable decade of the 1990s, we experienced tremendous prosperity. Literally overnight, we went from all to nothing. This transition was so thorough and swift, Peter and I could not miss its magnitude. There was no slow sinking into a gradual recession—it was a sudden and complete halt.

This economic disintegration occurred in three parts. First came the fall of the NASDAQ market. Much of our business had been in the institutional equity markets, however, our bond market clients minimized our losses through this time. We were prepared for such a slowdown. Nothing, however, could have prepared us for the second part of the assault. Not until September 11, in our wildest imagination, could we have conceived of an act of war directed right at Wall Street. For us, it was what the military calls a "direct hit." As we scrambled through the next few months to recreate some semblance of our former lives, the third and final blow to our economy unfolded with the unending trail of corporate and Wall Street scandals.

As we limped along as casualties of war, there was no mistaking the message: *we're going down*. Each time we rebuilt our business, something else hit us from another direction. When our transition was complete, we saw the world from a different perspective. Instead of from the top down, we viewed the world from the bottom up. This was a lesson in humility we could not ignore. In this humble state, something new emerged. Normally we were so focused on making money, we could not pause for a moment. But now we had time to reflect on the meaning of our lives.

The Difference a Day Makes

On the day of the attack, Peter and I were separated from each other and our children. Peter arrived at our midtown office as usual around 6:30 a.m. Our teenage son continued on to his private high school near Lincoln Center. Our daughter was at college two hours away. I dropped our youngest son off at kindergarten at 8:00 a.m. and began the forty-five-minute drive into the city. Halfway there I realized I left my wallet at home and turned back to get it. Now I was really late. I still wasn't used to the commute from our Long Island home. We had lived in the city for years and, for the sake of our youngest son, had recently moved full-time to our weekend home on Long Island's south shore.

As I walked into the house at 8:50 a.m., the phone rang. It was my sister-in-law from Montclair, New Jersey.

"Oh good, you're home," she said in a breathless voice. "Did you hear what happened?"

"No," I replied.

"Turn on the news."

I did so and saw the smoke pouring out of the World Trade Center. I got scared. "Where's Rob?" I asked. My brother arrived at One World Trade Center every morning between 8:30 and 8:45 a.m.

"He's home. The baby kept us up all night and he stayed to help me this morning. Where's Peter?"

"He's at the office. I have to call him."

Peter was in his normal work mode when I reached him. "Honey, I'm really busy right now. I have someone holding on another line and two meetings this morning back-to-back. What's up? Where are you?"

"A small plane hit the World Trade Center. They think it was a private plane that went off course."

"Was anyone hurt?"

"I don't know."

"I don't have time for this now. I have to go."

"Okay. I'll call you back when I know more."

"You're not coming in?"

"I'm not sure. I want to see if this will tie up traffic."

I did not want to leave my young son at school until I knew I could get home that evening. As I watched the news reports, I looked at my schedule to see how I could rearrange things. I still thought it was just a terrible accident. Then the second plane hit. Panic shot through me. "Oh, my God, we are being attacked!" I shouted to no one.

I called Peter. "Another plane hit the Towers. You have to leave."

"What are you talking about? I'm busy right now."

"Turn on CNN. We're being attacked."

"Alright. Alright. Calm down."

"Charles is at school. I have to call him," I started sobbing.

"Honey, just calm down."

"You don't understand. New York is being attacked! Two planes hit the Towers. That's not an accident. There might be more coming. You have to get Charles and get out!"

"Okay, I will turn on the news. Call Charles and call me back."

There was no answer on our older son's cell phone. No answer at his school. I called our office. No answer. I called my sister-in-law in Montclair. "All circuits are busy." I called Peter's cell phone. No answer. I called again. No answer. Three more tries and I finally got through to him.

"I can't believe this," Peter said.

"Please don't leave the office until you know what's going on."

"I won't. I love you."

"I love you too."

I did not want to hang up the phone. Yet all my motherly instincts told me to bring our little boy home. When I arrived at his school, the secretary was hysterical. Her husband was a firefighter in downtown New York. She had not heard from him. We hugged each other. Relief hit me when I saw my happy child. "Hi, Mommy. Are we going somewhere?" I drove home and tried to act normal, as fear for the safety of my husband and son filled me. "Go ahead and play, honey. I want to watch the news."

I will never forget the feelings of dread I felt that day. I stayed alone with my young son, watching the attack on television, cut off from everyone I knew. Except for my brother and sister-in-law and a few others, our closest family and friends were in New York City. I was glad my little son was safe with me outside the city. Only I could not stop thinking of Peter and Charles. "What if something happens to them?" I prayed for their safety. I prayed for the safety of the firemen we knew. I had not heard from Mark. He planned to go to Vermont that week. I hoped he made it. I could not get through to him or any of our other friends or relatives. All phone service in New York City was dead. Manhattan had been my home for twenty-two years. I fought an overwhelming urge to be there with my husband, son, friends and family.

I waited for word from Peter. Thoughts kept flooding my mind. "Please, bring him home safe." I could not imagine what life would be like without him. My husband was my best friend. We raised our children together, ran our business together and shared all aspects of our life. "Mommy, why are you crying? Is Daddy okay?" "Yes, honey. It's nothing. Go back and play." "Can we go to the beach?" "No, honey. Not today."

As the buildings crumbled on the small screen, I prayed for everyone I knew and those I didn't. Every family that just lost a loved one. Every firefighter, everyone on Wall Street, every single person in my beloved city. *What must they have endured?* I thought of the helpless people on the planes as they were forced to meet their terrifying ends. I thought of the innocents trapped in the Towers faced with choosing to jump to their deaths or burn alive. I could not get their images out of my head. *What kind of human beings would do something like this?* I prayed for our city and our country. *This must be what it's like in war.* "God bless America," I repeated to myself over and over. For the first time in my life, I fully understood that phrase. For me, September 11 will always be a day of prayer. I will never forget that day. The fear. The horror.

Peter walked the forty blocks to West 60th Street and retrieved our oldest son from his school lockdown. We were fearful that more planes would be attacking as the day went on. The city was shut down to anyone going or coming. "New York City closed," flashed the signs outside the city. No trains or buses were allowed in or out. All tunnels and bridges were closed. Air Force jets flew over the buildings. As so many others and I waited for news from our loved ones, an eerie quiet filled the streets in the suburbs around me. Peter and Charles turned our midtown apartment into a bunker. They stayed put for hours until the city officials allowed anyone to leave. When we were finally reunited, we held each other tight. Then we turned to hear the news of who was alive and who was dead.

A SHATTERED ILLUSION

After these events, our priorities shifted. Our focus on material success was suddenly replaced with a tremendous gratitude for our lives. For so many years, we had worked from one goal to the next. Every time we made a deal, we took no time to rest. We were motivated by the fear that it was never enough. We couldn't slow down. Many people saw the way we lived and thought, "How lucky they are." Only we never saw it that way. We were filled with constant anxiety. No matter how much money we made, we needed more.

We would never have stopped this frantic activity except when our business was ripped away from us. We were left only with the heart of our life: our children, our home, and our love for each other. This terrible event shattered the illusion we held for so long that we needed more than we already had. We realized we had everything we could possibly want right now. We watched the agony of those who lost their husbands, wives, daughters, sons, fathers, mothers, lovers and protectors. We thought of how blessed we were to have each other. Our hearts filled with gratitude. We needed nothing more.

UNNECESSARY SUFFERING

All of us asked that day, "Who are these people that want to destroy us? What have we ever done to make them hate us so?" Devoted parents. Recent college grads. Grandparents waiting for their pensions. Lovers and fiancés. Husbands of mothers-to-be. Future statesmen. All gone with these senseless acts. We did not even know our assailants, never saw them coming, never knew they were our enemies. It was the random violence of criminal minds. The city reeled from the deliberate cruelty of a small group of strangers. They celebrated our misery. Their indifference to our suffering was unfathomable.

The Aftermath

We had two renovation projects going at the time of the attack—one in East Hampton and one in midtown Manhattan. The East Hampton property was due to be sold the week of the attack. We worried the sale wouldn't go through. We needed the capital now. It was clear our search business would suffer.

The second project we had under way was a cooperative apartment renovation in midtown. One of the members of our crew, Patrick, was a firefighter who had been trapped under the World Trade Center for hours after the attack. Finally rescued, he detailed his daring escape to us. He had crawled through the debris not able to see his hand in front of him, due to the clouds of poisonous dust and smoke. Somehow he saw a sliver of light and found his way to freedom. However, the firefighters he went in with never came out. Afterward, he wasn't the same.

The next-door neighbor of one of our crew lost his firefighter brother in the attack. They had been close their whole lives. For six months after the burial, he watched the videotaped funeral over and over dressed in his brother's bunker gear. Friends and family were worried. They didn't want to lose him too.

When we heard of Father Mike's death immediately after the attack, things really hit home. Father Mychal Judge was the epitome of love and compassion. He and Peter had been friends for many years. "He couldn't have been killed," we thought. But it was confirmed. He had gone downtown with Engine 1/Ladder 24 to the site that morning to offer support. He, along with six of the firemen in that firehouse, perished in the early hours of September 11.

Every day we heard of new losses. An old friend called from Los Angeles a few days later. "Did you hear about Paddy Brown?" I held my breath. "He's gone?" "Yes." We were overcome with sadness. A deeply caring and honorable person, Captain Patrick Brown was the kind of man that came to mind when you thought of a hero. Self-effacing, compassionate and brave. It was not a surprise that he was one of the first firemen at Ground Zero that day. The list of our Wall Street colleagues was equally dramatic. We heard of more losses for a year afterward.

And Then There Were None

Our search business was at a standstill. There were huge numbers of people in our industry out of work. Our firm helped businesses grow by filling their top-level positions, yet now none of our clients needed our services. No firm was growing its business. They were letting people go by the thousands. One of our main clients told us, "There are so many people out of work; we can get anyone we want ourselves." We had worked exclusively for this firm for several years. Half the people there were personal friends. There was nothing they could do. There was a moratorium on search services direct from top management. In our experience, even in recession times, business grew in some areas. When the equity markets were down, bond markets were booming and vice versa. Suddenly, no one was doing any new business. We had never experienced this phenomenon before.

Many of our long-term friends and associates were being laid off. One firm used the term "restructuring" for the firing of thousands of workers. This was essentially a layoff, only the employer did not wish to call it that. They gave their employees a choice to take a severance package, or interview for "another job" which may or may not exist. Most people took the severance package. This way the firm saved themselves a lot of bad press, avoiding headlines like, "One of the world's most profitable investment banks lays off thousands two weeks after the attack on New York. Top managers keep their jobs."

It was always about image on Wall Street. If massive layoffs were made public, investors would get scared. The unspoken code declared "never let them see you sweat." It was truly survival-of-the-fittest now. Managers that had worked for the same firm for five, ten and fifteen years found themselves unemployed in the worst job market ever in New York since the Depression. A friend from Merrill Lynch said, "It feels like Armageddon." The only thing to do was grab onto the reins and go for the ride. There was no telling how long this would go on.

A Changing Climate

Many friends of ours in the industry who were not caught in the layoffs left their firms anyway. People had such profound experiences due to the attack, they had to make a change. Whatever they had planned to do years in the future, they did now. One managing director quit and spent a year volunteering with Habitat for Humanity. Another left Wall Street and sailed around the world with his family. The wife of a senior investment banker begged her husband not to return to Wall Street after the attack for the sake of their five children. He didn't. Two senior officers at another investment bank started consulting businesses out of their homes. They wanted to be close to their families and find time for the things they could never do before. Some of our associates had more than enough personal resources and retired from the business completely. Others used their wealth to create their own hedge funds or smaller investment firms.

It was a Wall Street in transition. Peter and I were sure about two things. Firstly, nothing lasts forever, either good or bad. Therefore, it was just a matter of time before these market conditions reversed. Secondly, business, like life, is in a constant state of change. In order to flourish, you must change with it.

All Bets Are Off

Fortunately, we had real estate income to balance our Wall Street losses. We put another property up for sale. Not a lot of people in the city were buying property in the spring of 2002. We managed to sell ours anyway. Against the advice of our accountant, we used the funds to pay our staff and maintain our office for the next few quarters. Our financial advisor had recommended we lay off beloved employees. There was little business in the foreseeable future in our industry. The long lines at the Madison Square Garden job fair and the dozens of phone calls from desperate candidates convinced us otherwise. We loved our staff. We spent years looking for good people and finally found them. Besides, where were they going to go in this job market? We were determined to keep them on as long as we could.

Six months after the attack, a few deals that were on the table in early September 2001 were resurrected again. However, it was a very different economic environment. One of the deals involved the placement of a senior manager that our client had been trying to hire for two years. It was considered a significant coup in the industry, as she was an important player in her field. Only now the hiring firm had the market wide open to them, and just before making her an offer, the hiring manager changed the terms of our contract. He offered us one-third of our prearranged fee. "That's not our deal," Peter reminded him. He replied, "I understand that. But if we don't hire her, you won't get paid anything."

We had a long and valued relationship with this firm. They always acted honorably. But after September 11, the upper management of the firm quietly changed hands. Old managers were pushed out in the subsequent corporate bloodbath.

For ten years, we worked for this firm on a retained basis. They would pay a portion of the fee up front as a retainer and the balance of the fee upon closing the deal. Suddenly with the new management that arrangement ended. They offered us a new contract based on contingency only. In this unpredictable market, we could only conduct our searches for them with no guarantees of payment or even a commitment to hiring anyone. Another challenging aspect of the new contract was the substitution of the replacement clause for a refund policy: if anyone we placed at the firm left for any reason whatsoever within a year, we must refund the full fee to them. (The firm laid off thousands of people in the first year after the attack.) Our prior agreement was that if a person quit or was fired for cause, not market conditions, we would replace them at no additional cost.

All this cost cutting by our old client seemed reasonable in the devastated economy until the end of the following fiscal year. Peter spoke to one of his friends in senior management as bonuses were being dispensed. "How did you do?" "I did all right," the co-head of the desk said. "They paid me seven million." This was an increase in salary of two million over the year preceding the attack.

In one of the worst years in the history of Wall Street, the investment bank had laid off over 3,000 people to cut expenses. At the same time, the firm's remaining top management gave themselves a 40% pay increase. That's just the way it is on Wall Street. Only the strongest survive.

No Honor Among Thieves

Within a few months after the attack on New York, the business community attacked itself. It began with Enron and the outrageous bankruptcy in the wake of its corporate officers' stock bailout. Senior executives made sure they took care of themselves before the company stock sank to nothing. Long-time employees and investors lost their entire savings because of the acts of a handful of men. This event was followed by a string of corporate debacles, culminating in the fall of WorldCom. It hit our industry hard and we personally felt the blows. This financial disaster rocked our economy more than anything that had come the year before. We were still reeling from our losses when the news erupted. In economic terms, it felt like another 9/11, without the body counts. Many businesses like ours lost millions in revenue and capital due to the attack. Now we lost more.

Bernie Ebbers, the founder and CEO of WorldCom, didn't feel his multimillion-dollar salary was enough. He needed more and it didn't seem to matter who he had to step over to get it. Praying for Jesus' help before the day's work began, he pilfered shareholder money without a hint of irony. He instructed his board of directors to give him a "loan" of $400 million. His "loan" would not look like salary or theft on paper. But theft it was—as it was taken directly from the pockets of others. He fed on the wounded carcass of WorldCom until it collapsed under the weight of his appetite. Fraud of some $11 billion and the company's subsequent bankruptcy exposed his economic cannibalism. It was the biggest accounting fraud in the history of American capitalism, and shockwaves reverberated throughout the western world.

Ebbers had two sides he showed to the public. One personality showered the Clinton, Missouri community he lived in with multimillion-dollar gifts. Townspeople called him a "fine Christian man" known for sharing with others. Some residents in Clinton described him as a "hometown hero." Even after his conviction, supporters still cling to the hope that he was just an innocent pawn in the middle of a pack of vipers. They want to believe the man they thought of as honorable and devoted to his community was real, even if others believe that he was only "out for himself." Why would someone as wealthy and respected as Ebbers need to rape and pillage his own company, devastate his hometown, cripple his country's economy and steal millions of other people's money? We may never know the answer for why seemingly good people succumb to incomprehensible acts of greed.

According to one major newspaper, "WorldCom's failure wiped out billions of dollars in money belonging to shareholders and employees. Thousands of employees lost their jobs in the aftermath." It hit the rest of the economy and millions of innocent bystanders pretty hard too.

Winner Takes All

The Wall Street analyst scandals followed WorldCom's fall. Just like some of their corporate brothers and sisters, a group of Wall Street experts had consistently satisfied their own needs at huge cost to others. Their gain was our loss. Entire dreams for the future were wiped out by the calculated deception of a small group of strangers. As Wall Street veterans, we knew not to take analysts' proclamations to heart. Not because anyone told us this, but simply because of the nature of their jobs. Analysts work for investment banks who subsequently serve businesses by underwriting their IPOs. A conflict of interest was built into the analyst's calls. Didn't the rest of the world watching know that? This is why we personally trusted our real estate investments more than the stock market. An associate and New York lawyer joined a class action suit against a large investment bank because his broker gave him false advice. We wondered how a Columbia-educated lawyer from New York could be duped by a broker. Stock market investment is gambling—plain and simple. It's like an amateur sitting down at a poker table with seasoned pros. You are going to get eaten alive. These people know how to bluff—this is what they are paid for. It was the gluttony and greed of the analysts combined with the gluttony and greed of investors that brought the markets down, and we all paid the price.

With the tumble of the markets went years of savings for millions of people. Wedding plans, down payments for homes, funds for stress-free golden years—all gone. A seventy-four-year-old neighbor of ours lost his retirement money with the WorldCom stock crash. He sold his family home of thirty-five years to make ends meet. The suicide of a North Shore Long Island couple was explained with a note, "We're ruined." The scandals did not cease—Adelphia, Tyco and pristine firms like Arthur Anderson were revealed for fraud. We saw "experts" on the financial news fabricating earnings reports, we read about them in business journals and lauded them for their acumen. Some prayed publicly, before they deceived their own colleagues. All the time, we never saw it coming, never knew they were our enemies. Their indifference to human suffering was difficult to comprehend.

Every Man for Himself

Our stock market let us down. Our defense systems failed us. Now our own people betrayed us. Who could we possibly trust anymore? Not only did we have to deal with death on Wall Street and the death of American innocence, we had to wrestle with the end of American business as we knew it.

As far back in history as we can look, there are people that, given the opportunity, would take everything and anything that wasn't nailed down. Still, we were shocked when some corporate and Wall Street executives did the same. Perhaps we were stunned by the magnitude of their thefts. Some people lost everything because a handful of individuals needed money to sponsor things like private hunting grounds and multimillion-dollar birthday parties. The level of gluttony was obscene by any standards—because money was taken from the personal savings of others. People's lives were irrevocably changed because of the actions of a self-serving few.

But with those acts of greed, they stole more than money; they robbed us of trust. What remained was a loss of faith in each other. Here was capitalism at its worst, a primitive, self-absorbed capitalism that destroyed everything in its path—a capitalism that deeply horrified us.

In his July 16, 2002 testimony to Congress, Federal Reserve Chairman Alan Greenspan said, "An infectious greed seemed to grip much of our business community." A devout capitalist, he detailed how greed adversely affects our economy. "Our market system depends critically on trust—trust in the word of our colleagues and trust in the word of those with whom we do business. Falsification and fraud are highly destructive to free-market capitalism and, more broadly, to the underpinnings of our society." Anyone listening understood his words. The foremost economic expert in the United States warned that unrestrained greed was dangerous to our economic system. He further connected it with the health and welfare of our entire society.

These warnings defied the glamorous view of corruption and greed we often held in the past. Less than fifteen years before the Fed chairman's wise words were spoken, greed had been exalted in the movie *Wall Street*—inspiring the generation to come with the famous saying, "Greed is good." After lying low for a brief period following Black Monday in 1987, unbridled greed became fashionable again.

Causing harm to another should never be viewed as glamorous. In our modern world, full of unavoidable human suffering, we must look within ourselves for a deeper sense of social conscience. Because we have accepted that nothing we do in the pursuit of profit is "personal," we have often failed in business to connect our actions to the suffering of others. Greed is a human tragedy; it has many victims seen and unseen.

DEFINING GREED

A focus on building wealth is a personal thing to be determined within our individual moral frame of reference. A person's wealth is really no one's business other than his or her own. There should be no moral judgment on it. How does the wealth of another affect you personally? Is it taking anything away from you? Does it create envy, competition, inadequacy or admiration in you? These responses are much more a reflection of you than the individual you are observing. Wealth is simply the state of one's economic affairs. Everything else we add to this is a projection of our own needs. Whether we buy a shower curtain costing $6,000 or $6 is a personal choice—nothing more, nothing less, except of course if we are not using our own money.

As a culture we often mistake the simple pursuit of wealth for greed. We assume a person's wealth is accumulated at the expense of someone else. Individuals gain wealth every day without taking from others. If we define greed as the taking of money or objects at the expense of others then we can understand that greed and wealth accumulation are two separate things. Wealth is our personal affair; greed becomes a public concern. Thomas Aquinas, the thirteenth-century theologian, called greed, "A sin directly against one's neighbor, since one man cannot over-abound in external riches, without another man lacking them." In the days of serfs and lords this was surely true. In modern entrepreneurial America where individuals create wealth daily using their own hard work and creative resources, this is no longer valid.

The multimillionaire inventor Dean Kamen is a wonderful example of this. A few years back on the news show *60 Minutes*, he said, "I hope I put more into the world than I take out." There are many people of wealth who earn it with their own mental and physical resources. Assuming individuals are wealthy because they stole from others is not accurate. In

Kamen's case, it's quite the contrary. Kamen has significantly contributed to other people by ingenious inventions like the IBOT, a robotic wheelchair that climbs stairs.

Like Aquinas, we may confuse greed with creating wealth. According to the American Heritage Dictionary, *greed* is "the excessive desire for more than one needs." This means that we do not have to *possess* more than we need to be greedy, just *desire* it. But what one needs is so subjective that unless we live in a tent around an open fire, this might include most of us. Greed is not simply having more than others; greed implies a desire for money that harms others in the pursuit of it. As the recent prosecutions of cold-hearted corporate officers reveal, greed is an act "against one's neighbor" when we employ destructive means. When we exhibit greed, we are not thinking of anyone else but ourselves. Pure self-interest has replaced any semblance of human compassion we might otherwise have.

DIVINE RIGHT

In 2005, *USA Today* reported, "The era of CEO pay packages befitting royalty still reigns." CEO pay structure represents the ever-widening gap between the average worker and management. What used to be around a 20:1 ratio is now closer to 500-1000:1. Mid-level employees earning between $50,000 and $100,000 annually can read about their CEO receiving $50 million in annual compensation. An analyst for the shareholder watchdog group, The Corporate Library remarks, "Forget restraint. After years of moderate gains, it's business as usual." Multibillionaire investor Warren Buffet has an annual compensation of $350,000 as head of one the world's most profitable conglomerates. He calls excessive CEO pay "obscene."

Is getting paid a lot of money for what you do well "obscene," or is it the American dream? Sports stars are paid enormous sums and fans mumble about their greed. Yet they routinely line up to buy tickets that pay these inflated salaries. Aren't middle-class people attending seminars and buying books on how to get rich in record numbers? How many millions of hopefuls play the lottery every week? How many winners give the money back? Obviously being rich is not the problem. The issue to be examined in terms of CEO pay is the "accumulation of money at the expense of others." Because CEO salaries are paid from other people's money, they are under constant scrutiny.

Alan Greenspan claimed the practice of tying CEO pay to stock options was "ripe for corruption." William McDonough, former president of the New York Federal Reserve Bank, declared it a "terribly bad social policy and perhaps even bad morals."

What started out as a great idea in the 1990s to inspire normally risk-adverse managers to ever greater profits has backfired to a large degree on members of the industry. Options-for-pay was originally intended as a reward for genuine growth, and corporate executives have been "on their honor" to win this award legitimately. In a study at the University of Washington Business School, the assistant professor of business ethics Scott Reynolds found that for some people the ends justify the means. He discovered that this kind of individual was not particularly sensitive to the ethical or moral issues of how to arrive at the end result. Reynolds speculated that the Enron CEO and his colleagues were "ends-focused" individuals blinded to any ethical concerns by the bottom line. Enron's former CFO Andy Fastow said of his illegal actions to inflate stock value, "I believe I was extremely greedy and lost my moral compass and I've done terrible things that I regret." Tyco CEO Dennis Kozlowski was convicted along with his chief financial officer, Mark Schwartz, of stealing $120 million from the company and its shareholders and pocketing another $575 million from stock manipulations.

Cruel abuses like these litter our economic landscape and destroy the climate for remaining managers who would not dream of doing such things. Enron and WorldCom's great accounting scams resulted in punishing the entire corporate world. The Sarbanes-Oxley Act was legislated to prevent falsifying earnings in public companies. Although created for an honorable purpose, this act is thought to be the bane of existence for some otherwise ethical accounting departments. Thousands of hours of tedious paperwork add huge financial and labor burdens to internal corporate governance. All because of the outsized greed of a handful of top managers.

Show Me the Money

Many corporate officers who manage companies for a couple of years walk away with multiple millions in severance even after stock values sink during their tenure. Pension fund investors are suing former Hewlett-Packard directors for the "excessive" severance pay of $42 million to terminated CEO Carly Fiorina. A risky and much protested merger with Compaq, "Fiorina's Folly" cost the company hundreds of millions of dollars in value and thousands of jobs for individuals. The economic fallout will be felt for years to come. Shareholders are demanding some of her compensation be returned. HP referred to their policy of paying departing CEOs no more than 2.99 times their annual salary. Since when do we pay anyone for diminishing value to a product or service? Would we pay the average worker three times her salary for failing to perform her job? Why would we do this for a CEO?

This has created shareholder backlash when large payouts are made to executives of failing or bankrupt companies. In 2003, Delta Air Lines' top management set aside a pension fund of $45 million for themselves while under funding worker pensions by $5 billion. Similarly, senior executives at

American Airlines' parent corporation, AMR Corp., were exposed for creating a separate retirement program for themselves shortly before they asked workers to give up retirement benefits. CEO Donald Carty publicly apologized for this inequity but was later forced to resign.

One of the most outrageous misuses of executive power was the pay package of $140 million for the former chairman and CEO of the New York Stock Exchange, Richard Grasso, two years after September 11. Even Big Board members and heads of investment banks were repulsed by this untimely gluttony which included a bonus of $5 million for reopening the exchange following the attacks. *BusinessWeek* wrote in late 2003, "While the ability of the exchange to start functioning again after the terrorist attacks was remarkable, so was the performance of the firefighters, police, and thousands of other New Yorkers." None of these heroes were paid a bonus. The outcry in the midst of continued national and citywide recovery was enormous.

You've Got a Friend

There are also CEOs out there who tip the scale in the other direction. Best Buy's CEO, Bradbury Anderson, says he is "not trying to do a great thing" by handing over nearly a million of his personal stock options to hourly workers. According to the *Wall Street Journal* in December 2005, the ex-stereo salesman said, "I'm just trying to do what is appropriate as a leader." A Best Buy cashier who was awarded 200 of Anderson's shares responded, "This is not his company. It is our company, and he appreciates the job that we do."

Former Telecom CEO, Leo Hindery, author of *It Takes a CEO: It's Time to Lead with Integrity*, states that "excessive executive and CEO compensation belies the principles of meritocracy" and establishes management as "something akin to royalty." Best Buy's Anderson sums up the practice of sharing the wealth with workers by saying that if CEOs want to push workers harder they must "walk the talk."

LIBERTY AND JUSTICE FOR ALL

So great is the public outrage over pay abuses that lawmakers are writing legislation to allow shareholders voting rights for executive compensation. Laws can't be expected to safeguard any of us from the excesses of individual greed. The need for self-governance among corporate executives is urgent. What rules can we apply to be "spiritually correct" as money managers? As we serve ourselves are we accountable to others? Have we earned our money fairly and reasonably without taking what rightfully belongs to someone else? Good leaders should be willing to sacrifice along with the people they lead. We teach our children to play "fair" and "by the rules" and often as otherwise responsible adults, we can't manage this ourselves. What we teach our children publicly in all areas of personal conduct should be the basic rules for ourselves in business.

A poll of the Sexiest Jobs of 2006, compiled by AOL and Salary.com, revealed a firefighter as the top choice for those surveyed and CEO following directly behind. Moving beyond the obvious superficiality, we discover a deeper underlying message. A CEO represents money and authority while a firefighter represents integrity and compassion. If we join these elements together, we understand the most compelling job qualities one could have as a CEO are money and authority combined with integrity and compassion.

JUDGE NOT

Acts of greed are not restricted to Wall Street and the corporate world. Greed is a human trait. It knows no economic or social boundaries. Wall Street has more money concentrated in one area than most industries. Therefore, there is more opportunity for greed. However, after two decades on Wall Street, we discovered there is no more greed there than anywhere else. From Hale House to Jim and Tammy Faye Bakker to Enron, it permeates all levels of society. Whether it's the clerk at the corner store who tips the deli scale with a finger or two, the doctor who uses patient quotas for billing at the expense of proper medical care or the car mechanic who fixes something that isn't broken, greed takes all forms.

Perhaps we are all partially responsible for acts of greed in our society. As a culture, we have an underlying conflict in our relationship to money. We are repulsed by greed, but fascinated with wealth. If society grants us its most coveted status solely on our wealth, then the message is to get rich at any cost. In the wake of September 11, our vanity culture seemed absurd next to the images of the brave firefighters, police, ironworkers, medical community, our mayor and the everyday New Yorkers who came to the rescue. These individuals were prized by us not for their wealth, but for their honor. On that day, all the distractions we inundate ourselves with daily were forgotten. Celebrity worship, sports obsessions, reality TV, movie star gossip, music videos, shopping, fashion trends, makeovers, techno toys, vanity pursuits of all kinds and the rest of our momentary pleasures disappeared in the wake of a powerful human experience. Our trauma magnified our priorities. Our stock portfolios and market calls were secondary to concern for each other. The challenge for each of us is to find a way to integrate the lessons learned through our suffering into our everyday reality.

As business partners in a capitalistic structure, we value making money. However, it became clear to us in the last few years that our business community needs to develop a new code of behavior in pursuing profit. We must recognize how acts of greed affect others. No longer can we justify the unnecessary suffering our indifference creates. We can earn our money responsibly and not destroy anyone else in the process. In our desire for wealth, the cultural acceptance of greed must be replaced with a more *spiritual correctness*. We look for ways to lessen the hardship of others, rather than adding to it. The tremendous compassion we experienced in the wake of September 11 brought the business community together with the world around it. However, the acts of greed revealed afterward through the continuous scandals split us apart again. We must make a collective choice in business between destructive greed and creating wealth with a conscience. As the Wall Street community itself learned from the firefighters in that long difficult year, greed and honor cannot exist side by side.

◆

Lesson 3

Profit honorably without taking from others

> *"The greatest honor of a man is in doing good to his fellow men, not in destroying them."*
>
> THOMAS JEFFERSON
> AMERICAN PRESIDENT

Profit honorably without taking from others

THERE are two kinds of suffering in the world: necessary and unnecessary. Necessary suffering comes from the difficulties and losses we can't avoid, those outside of our control—the acts of a power greater than ourselves. These are the inevitable realities of life including illness, loss of loved ones and natural disasters. Unnecessary suffering is the suffering human beings create for each other and themselves. These events in our lives result from acts of deliberate human cruelty, neglect or selfishness. In the business world, we have witnessed much unnecessary suffering these past few years due to unrestrained greed. Otherwise respected businesspeople chose to profit at the expense of others.

It is important to examine what motivates us toward greed. Is it the perceived need for *more* at any cost? Is it the competitive compulsion to win, no matter what? Are we fully aware of how our acts of greed harm others? What kind of win is it anyway, if it is based on our exploiting people's weaknesses? What kind of winner are we really, if our spoils are taken from the fortunes and assets of another?

Greed is only possible in the absence of humility. If we remain humble and unafraid in our monetary affairs, the necessary shift away from greed can take place. True self-worth of our business acumen should be measured in more cogent terms. Perhaps we could give ourselves the challenge to win fair and square using our creative resources, rather than brute force. The mark of a truly accomplished businessperson is the achievement of monetary goals without hurting anyone else.

In our world, most gluttonous behavior is thought repulsive. For example, as a culture, we are critical if we eat too much or drink to excess. Yet there is little in our common psychology that would restrain us from devouring all the money we can find while harming others. As we view the current business debauchery, we need to develop a social and moral ethic against the excesses of greed. It is simply good business all the way around to establish this thinking. Instead of "winner takes all," we can begin to think of an ocean of abundance open to us that is capable of fulfilling all of our needs without denying the needs of anyone else.

KEY POINTS IN LESSON THREE

›   Gain at the expense of others is not a worthy "win."

›   The suffering you create for others and yourself is unnecessary suffering.

›   A genuine sense of security is based on personal character.

How Does Lesson Three Manifest in Your Business Life?

Example #1

President, Retail Brokerage Firm

An affable young businessman, with his middle-aged female partner, owns a multimillion-dollar securities firm servicing high-net-worth individuals. Both started in business with inherited wealth. Before he turned thirty, his parents gave the young man a substantial stock portfolio. The female partner enjoyed a legacy of great wealth and real estate from a long line of Boston blue-blood money.

The young man began at the firm as a rookie broker when his uncle, then a senior partner, encouraged him to come aboard. The young man and his new friend, the female junior partner, became frustrated with the uncle's penchant for ethics. They felt he needed to be a bit more cold-hearted with employees. Soon the young man saw greater opportunity, and with the woman's assistance, he maneuvered the uncle out in a successful takeover.

As partners, they seemed to work together well. The young man never questioned his new partner's creative arithmetic and they both increased their wealth substantially. They paid their workers with commission only and posted daily quota numbers for all to see on the wall.

Their business took a huge dive after the stock market crash of October 1987. It never occurred to them to use their personal wealth to pay their outstanding debts. Their solution was to leave their downtown office space on a Saturday afternoon, with many months' rent in arrears. Unfortunately for their employees and creditors, they left without notice and set up shop across the street under a slightly different corporate name. Although the woman partner did not have many close friends or family, the young man was quite different. Outside of business, he was a devoted father and a good husband, said to be an honorable and thoughtful man. Yet in business, he believed profits came before anything. Because of this view, he had great difficulty cultivating loyalty among clients and employees.

<hr />

EXAMPLE #2

PRESIDENT, FINANCIAL SERVICES AND MONEY MANAGEMENT FIRM

A midtown financial services firm had enjoyed several years of great success. Their reputation for excellence in ethics as well as financial expertise kept them top performers in their field. All of their business came from word-of-mouth referral. Many of the top echelon of the business world worked exclusively with them.

The firm was founded and run by a brilliant economist whose dynamic energy and refreshing brand of honesty earned him the trust of everyone he met. Not only gifted at creating wealth, he was also a deeply compassionate man. When clients were not doing well and couldn't pay him, he worked without billing them. He required no minimum investment or income for his time. He never turned anyone away and gave retired schoolteachers the same attention and expertise he gave to officers of Fortune 500 companies. When a cash-short client wanted to buy a home, he lent him the deposit. After another client hit a financial bottom, he offered them free office space until they got back on their feet. When the recession finally affected his firm, instead of laying off long-term employees, he re-mortgaged his house and used his own personal assets to pay their salaries for two years. "They depend on me," he said. "I can't let them down."

Applying Lesson Three to Your Life

When it comes to money, we are sometimes like starving animals in the wild. We devour all the money we can find, for fear we will find no more. We search for a quick killing and easy profit, without any thought to the carcasses we leave behind. As we collect our short-term profits, we may realize that in the long term we have sacrificed more than we gained. When we cause suffering for others for our own gratification, we stand to lose self-respect, peace of mind and the trust and support of others. In simple profit terms, we can be gaining at the moment, but substantially diminishing our returns over the long run.

Tools to Help Control the Desire for More in the Pursuit of Profit

› Separate your measure of self-worth from your net worth.

› Create wealth from personal achievement and avoid savagery.

› Strive for personal satisfaction and accomplishment through honorable activities.

Creating a Vision of Honor Over Greed

Choose not to use your desire for wealth, success and material possessions to cause suffering to anyone else. Pursue profits by using your creative abilities and not your lower nature. Be aware of how your behavior affects others. In your quest to win, always act honorably and for the highest good of all.

◆

Chapter 4

The Miracle

"*How selfish soever man may be supposed, there are evidently some principles in his nature, which interest him in the fortune of others, and render their happiness necessary to him, though he derives nothing from it except the pleasure of seeing it.*"

ADAM SMITH

ECONOMIST

The Miracle

THE extraordinary kindness expressed by millions of people across the country and the world to New York City in the aftermath of this horror helped ease the pain for many of us. It was truly gratifying to hear people proclaim, "We are all New Yorkers now." America rallied around us. We agonized together about the firefighters lost, the defenseless working people who perished in the Towers, the harrowing terror of those on the doomed planes and the inconceivable attack on the Pentagon. We were one in our shared grief. If we never knew what humanitarian people we were before, we knew now. Even individuals of practiced indifference responded with caring and concern.

New York was a very different place in those months afterward. Ordinarily raucous streets were oddly silent. Cars no longer honked their horns obsessively. They paused for pedestrians. This might sound strange to anyone outside of New York, but the city was home to an aggressive driving style only second to Rome. Even this ceased.

We offered our office and our home to anyone who might need it. We cooked dinners for neighboring firehouses, brought donuts and coffee to our local police and gave thermal clothes to the National Guard. We spent hours at Ground Zero, offering human comfort and an ear to listen to anyone who wanted it. All around us other New Yorkers and concerned visitors did these things too. Peter and I would walk into Engine 1, Ladder 24 on West 31st Street to pay our respects to Father Mychal and the six firemen this firehouse lost. Many others were doing the same. A memorial, with candles and photographs of the fallen, was created by well-wishers and set up outside the firehouse. There was always a crowd of people in front of the firehouse, praying and crying.

Firefighter Tim Brown, formerly a member of the renowned Rescue 3 in New York City, said he was moved by the extraordinary bravery and compassion of civilians to one another on September 11. As he navigated a rescue in Tower One before the collapse, ordinary New Yorkers were helping others out of the building—pregnant women, disabled persons, anyone who needed assistance. In an inspired act of unity, many of those running for their lives were not leaving anyone behind. Captain Al Fuentes whose miraculous rescue on 9/11 is detailed in chapter eight, wrote in his memoir, *American By Choice*, "We were all witnesses to a most wonderful and generous outpouring of love and support from all Americans during and after this disaster."

A Higher Calling

In our normally self-absorbed city, these acts of kindness became commonplace. In a city where 8 million live and millions more work or visit each day, New Yorkers learn to distance themselves. To maintain privacy, we keep to ourselves in elevators, stores and any other public place. However, the tragedy instantly changed that dynamic. Suddenly, New Yorkers of all different backgrounds responded openly to each other with sympathy and consideration. People from all over the country arrived just to lend a hand wherever they could. Overnight, out of our pain and suffering, the city and the country were transformed.

To much of the country, New York had a self-serving image. One theatergoer from a Connecticut suburb told a local news reporter after the attack, "They (New Yorkers) came down a few notches. They don't seem so full of themselves." America itself was often viewed this way by the rest of the world. Looking at the heartbroken masses, it was easy to see our humanity now. The tragedy revealed to everyone watching what a deeply caring people we were. Intolerance gave way to patience, indifference to concern. It took this monumental event to bring out the best in each of us. In a matter of hours, New Yorkers in huge numbers dropped their defenses and replaced them with compassion. We proved it could be done—it was truly a miracle.

Angels Among Us

People always respond to help each other when disasters of this magnitude occur. In tragedy, the masks we normally use to hide from others disappear. We are left only with our core selves as we focus on the more weighty issues of life and death. However, it seemed in these particular circumstances that we were more responsive to each other than usual. A cousin from Berlin said that the German people were holding candlelight vigils. A friend in Poland and another in Rome said people everywhere shared our suffering. Firehouses all over the world were in mourning for our firemen. The international community observed minutes of silence to honor those lost and to pray for America's pain.

Everyone was inspired by the acts of the firefighters. We were profoundly moved by those who went into the Towers to save victims and never came out and by those who continued to perform their jobs after their brothers perished. At a funeral for a veteran volunteer fireman in Long Island, the priest began his eulogy, "Firemen. What can we say about firemen? They're like Jesus." Through the firefighter, we see the true meaning of giving. They put aside their needs for ours. They push through their own fear and give up their comfort for us.

Most firefighters we know are gentle, loving people, angels among us who have arms of steel and hearts of gold. Each of them would give the shirt off his back anytime, anywhere, if you needed it. There is something that changes human beings when they spend their lives helping others. Not only does it bring out the best in others, it brings out the better part of them. We have known some firefighters personally who are as flawed as anyone else; yet no matter who they are and what they are like privately, when duty calls they leave their ordinary selves behind and become their best selves. Peter, who has traveled in ambulances on calls with firemen, says the toughest guy will become gentle and loving when comforting a frightened victim. They visibly change through the pure act of giving. A normally irritable chief at one of Long Island's volunteer firehouses changes immediately when he is asked about what he does. He says, "We are here to help people. That's what we're all about." In the line of duty, they make no judgments of who is worthy of their help. A firefighter doesn't ask what religion you are, who your parents are and who you voted for before he saves you. In the eyes of a firefighter, all lives are worthy.

In the Image of Firefighters

If you have ever experienced an emergency, you know the inexpressible gratitude felt on the receiving end of giving. Imagine being part of a head-on collision and becoming trapped inside your car, praying to get out alive. To your relief and amazement,

EMS and firefighters appear on the scene and cut you out of your car. They ask no questions and demand no reward.

In these moments, as we experience an intimacy that is beyond words, we are no longer strangers. There are no barriers between us. We look at our savior with an open heart, because this individual asks for nothing but gives his or her all. This exchange is the true nature of giving. It is remarkable that outside our major cities, most First Responders, firefighters and EMS personnel are volunteers who receive little compensation other than the satisfaction of helping others. We never forget our rescuer. The experience is personal and profound, reaffirming the basic humanity within us.

What happened on September 11 and in the months that followed was that all of us present and all of those watching were remade in the image of firefighters. In an extraordinary moment in time, we forgot our petty differences, personal desires and ambitions while engaged in the selfless act of helping others. In the process, each of us understood the reciprocal benefits of giving as fully as the rescue workers themselves. In those moments, we moved from our baser selves to our greater selves, and felt renewed by it.

We Reap What We Sow

Helping others is an essential part of our lives. It can be as simple as a kind word to the clerk in a store or holding the door open for the person behind us. It can be a prayer for someone who is suffering or a thoughtful gesture to a neighbor. We can give the car in front of us the right of way, buy lunch for a hungry stranger, thank the person delivering our mail or simply be gracious to others in our daily activities. The ways we can help each other are endless. They can be big, small or anything in between. Each gesture can make an enormous difference in a person's life.

After the tragedy, Peter and I were changed. We always considered ourselves thoughtful people and would gladly help anyone who asked. Only after 9/11, we no longer waited to be asked. Impatient as any other stressed-out New Yorker, we had a new tolerance for the needs of others. We walked differently, drove differently, talked differently. The whole world took on a new hue. We saw ourselves connected to everyone else. We saw that we could make a positive difference in the lives of others.

In the immediate aftermath of the attack, we made a point to thank every uniformed person we saw. Peter carried a sign in his car with THANK YOU written in large black letters and flashed it to every police officer and National Guardsman stationed by the tunnels. He walked up to a tough-looking policeman on a midtown corner. "I just want to say thank you for all you're doing. I appreciate it and everyone in the city does too." The hardened New York cop's demeanor softened. He was visibly moved and said, "No one ever thanked me before. I guess something good came out of this."

Two months after the attack, Peter felt he could no longer let others carry the load. He was inspired by those who helped us to help others. He volunteered for our local fire department on Long Island and has been an active member ever since. Since moving our home to New Jersey, he joined the Firefighter Assist Search Team and the First Responder Task Force in our community. He calls becoming a volunteer firefighter "one of the greatest experiences of my life." It has profoundly changed both our lives by showing us the spiritual importance of selflessness.

THE POWER OF GIVING

After the events of September 11, the most significant change in our cultural history was the extraordinary response from all sectors of civilian, corporate and religious communities to contribute to the victims. In America we have never seen such an outpouring of love and charity from every area of society. Individuals to Fortune 500 companies opened their wallets and gave all they could. It reverberated around the world even reaching deep into rural Africa. The Massai tribe in Kenya was so moved by the tragedy that they offered the U.S. their most valued possessions: cattle. "To the people of America, we give these cows to help you." The Massai tribal member who orchestrated the gift was attending Stanford University Medical School when he heard of the attack. He explained the tribe's extraordinary gesture by stating, "We cry for the pain of other people."

Well-wishers all over the world sent gifts of money and prayers. The Robin Hood Foundation, a group of invest-ment bankers devoted to eradicating poverty in New York, organized the Concert for New York City along with Eng-lish-born musician, Paul McCartney. Huge corporations like AOL and Miramax joined as sponsors along with dozens of world famous performers who donated their time and talent in solidarity with the wounded rescue workers. The monies raised by the foundation were given to the families of the fire-fighters and police officers killed in the attack. It was an event none of us in New York will ever forget.

The highly paid billionaire host of a popular television talk show, Oprah Winfrey, gave back to viewers in an un-precedented manner. She devoted countless shows to the vic-tims and their families, the First Responders, the volunteers, the unsung heroes and the entire scope of the human tragedy. Typically, talk shows are for-profit ventures that make money on limited agendas, celebrity gossip and sensationalism. On *Oprah*, the American public received expensive airtime devot-ed to ordinary people caught in extraordinary circumstances. The shows encouraged others to give their time, money and talent to those afflicted through a nonprofit branch of the program, the Angel Network. These efforts were repeated for victims of the tsunami in 2004 and Hurricane Katrina. The show's production company, Harpo Productions, found a balance between earning large profits and contributing to the public through service.

The Big Picture

There is a bigger picture, in which every business fits, and the larger the corporation, the bigger its scope. Some powerful companies in the United States insist their sole obligation is to profit. Their corporate officers routinely declare they owe the country little, as their priority is the bottom line. What if you said that to your children, friends or neighbors? "I only care for myself." Wouldn't you be thought savage? There is no separation between our monetary pursuits and our personal ones in terms of spiritual understanding. We are responsible for everything we do wherever and whenever we do it. We cannot use the anonymity of a corporate identity to shield us from that responsibility.

The Buddhists call this the Law of Karma. Christians follow the Golden Rule. Tzedakah is as fundamental to Judaism as Social Dharma is to Hinduism and Zakat is to Islam. All religious traditions include the practice of obligatory giving in their spiritual teachings. What you give to the world you create for yourself. What do we leave behind for others in our quest for profit? Are we improving the world or destroying it? If we are thoughtful, moral people, we must care about the world we create and the people in it. It is not just about me and what I want. It is also about you and what you want. In a world of one you can do as you please, but as soon as there are two, you must adjust to the other. This is basic spiritual logic.

Business is a social force with an inherent obligation to give back to the world it functions in. As individuals involved in large and small profit ventures, we must see ourselves in the big picture. We are our actions and our actions are us. Our acts of giving enhance those around us. In the process, we benefit as well. When we give we are no longer separate—we become one group working together. In giving, we uplift ourselves to a state of grace and love.

Tragedies like September 11 teach us that we are capable of rising above our lesser human selves and becoming like the angels among us. By using the collective memory of our response during that enormous disaster, we can consciously build a better society. In our hearts, we are each a little like a firefighter. By their example, we see what is possible for all of us to achieve: to give to others what we wish to receive. In doing so, we transform ourselves.

◆

Lesson 4

Giving to others is a gift for yourself

"It is one of the most beautiful compensations of life that no man can sincerely try to help another without helping himself."

RALPH WALDO EMERSON
PHILOSOPHER

Lesson 4

Giving to others is a gift for yourself

TO believe that business is all taking and no giving is to misunderstand the underlying purpose of business. Business is a reciprocal cycle of human effort. Supply and demand equals give and take. You receive rewards for creating useful and desirable products and services. In turn, you must replenish what you use of the system with an equal contribution. Many of us mistakenly take a "What's in it for me?" attitude. This thinking tremendously limits our experience. Changing that thought process to "How can I give out as much as I take in?" greatly expands your horizons.

The nature of your actions reverberates into the world and returns to you, even if you don't recognize it. It is what Buddhists call "cause and effect." This means that if you are selfish or miserly, you will experience this as a limitation in your own life. You will attract selfishness and selfish people to you. Conversely, if you are giving in thought and deed, you draw like behavior to you. In biblical terms, "As you reap, you will sow," or "Give and it will be given unto you."

Some might say, "I need to take care of myself." Of course, but there is a vast difference between selfishness and self-preservation. Selfishness implies an overdeveloped self-absorption and inhibits your individual growth and potential. You are so focused on your own needs that you cannot see those of others. Self-preservation, however, is serving yourself in a nurturing way, allowing you to recognize the needs of others as you care for yourself.

You might at times demand "I want" without any thought to what others may want. Then you wonder why you are having difficulty finding true intimacy. Selfishness can stifle any possibility of a deeper connection to others. It is the product of an underdeveloped thought process. In children, this lesson can be seen clearly. Children playing together at young ages will often say, "You can't have that, it's mine!" As grown-ups, our job is to teach them the concepts of sharing. Some children find learning to share easy. For others, it is more difficult—and so it is for adults. But as a child develops into teenage years and then into early adulthood, hopefully a transformation occurs. A child's world is centered on the self. She is the center of her own universe. As she grows and absorbs more of the outside world into her consciousness, this view begins to include others.

The process of spiritual maturation involves understanding that you are not the center of the universe. There are many universes in your life that intersect with all the people you meet. If you are loath to give to others and insist on focusing your attention solely on yourself, you cut yourself off from a more enriching life experience. If you learn to expand your view to include the views of others, your world expands.

Concern for others is not simply a charitable notion, but a necessary component in our continued existence. If we include a concern for others in all that we do, including our business affairs, the world around us would change. In turn, we reap the benefits of increased harmony in our surroundings. Indifference leaves us empty. Empathy returns us to love. Each of us is part of the common human experience: we breathe to live, we bleed when we are cut, we grieve when our loved one dies. These simple truths make us more the same than different. It is not us *versus* them; it is us *and* them. Therefore, concern for others is concern for yourself as well.

Business needs to give because it takes. Giving back in business is not an elective but an obligation. We need to replenish the community we have depleted for our own gain—it is a necessary action to balance the spiritual scales. All taking and no giving does not serve us any better than all giving and no taking would. If we give the shirt off our backs in business or in other areas of our life, then we freeze ourselves. Yet if we care for our needs and our own profits and then include giving, we serve two masters: our economic bottom line and our spiritual bottom line.

KEY POINTS IN LESSON FOUR

› The nature of your actions reverberates into the world and returns to you.

› Concern for others is concern for yourself.

› When you include others in your view, your world expands.

› Business needs to give because it takes.

HOW DOES LESSON FOUR MANIFEST IN YOUR BUSINESS LIFE?

EXAMPLE #1

OWNER, INTERNATIONALLY FAMOUS NIGHTCLUB

After inheriting a popular nightspot from her late husband, this new nightclub owner quickly forgot her work-

ing-class roots. Back in the days when she worked as a cocktail waitress at the club, she could often be heard discussing management's shortcomings. Yet upon becoming management herself, her sympathy for both customers and workers ceased. Each customer was now an opportunity for exploitation. One of the first things she did as an owner was double the cover charge, much to the dismay of her club's loyal clientele. When none of them returned, she was unconcerned, reasoning that there would always be new customers. Although long-time employees had contributed substantially to her livelihood, she thought of them as irritations. No more of the paid vacations or health insurance her dead husband had given them. During her first Christmas as a club manager, she showed off her newly purchased jewelry and cashmere coat to everyone she saw. Yet when it came time for bonuses, there was nothing in the till. She let two beloved workers go with no severance pay. They received only the message, "I don't need you anymore" on their answering machines. All the people in her life were completely expendable to her, except for the celebrities with whom she tried to surround herself.

Somehow in her self-reverie, she didn't notice that the manager she hired to care for her business was pocketing every available dollar he could. It was no surprise that a few years later, she lost the entire business due to bankruptcy. Her life was bankrupt, too, with no friends, family, or home of her own. From her million-dollar business, surrounded by supporters and her huge West Village loft, she was left with nothing. She found herself living in a small rent-subsidized apartment without enough money to pay for a telephone.

EXAMPLE #2

HEAD OF GLOBAL FIXED INCOME SALES, TOP TIER INVESTMENT BANKING FIRM

A managing director at one of the top investment banking firms on Wall Street was so loved by his employees that hundreds of them wept when he retired. For twelve years, he ran the firm as one of the top corporate officers. Along with two colleagues, he set the tone for the firm of honesty and fairness. Theirs was a respected Wall Street trading firm that followed two basic tenets: they did not deceive their clients and employees were valued as much as the bottom line. He believed that if his employees were happy, the business would profit and flourish. Staffers were not afraid to tell him of their complaints or needs. He gave everyone a fair chance to work to his or her capacity. People rarely left the company and business boomed. He made unprecedented deals on a handshake and never went back on his word. It was with great regret that his firm wished him farewell.

The thing that surprised everyone was why he was retiring at such a young age. He had made all the millions he needed to never have to work again, but most men in his position don't find it easy to give up that kind of money and power.

At age fifty-two, he decided to fulfill a life-long dream. He created a nonprofit foundation funneling Wall Street millions into helping economically disadvantaged children get a fighting chance to succeed. He spends his own money and that of his former colleagues, teaching children in impoverished urban neighborhoods how to build financially and professionally satisfying futures.

Applying Lesson Four to Your Life

Jesus spoke of the Golden Rule: "Do unto others, as you would have them do unto you." A few hundred years earlier, Confucius said, "Never do to others what you would not like them to do to you." These spiritual truths hold the same power for our personal growth today as they did when they were written. In modern terms, "Give what you wish to receive."

Tools to Include Giving in Your Work and Business Activities

› Treat others as you wish to be treated.

› To give is as important as it is to receive.

› Every action you take in life will return to you in one form or another.

Creating a Vision of Balance Between your Spiritual and Work Life

Include giving to others in your daily tasks. Treat all those around you as you wish to be treated by them. Give up self-focus by putting your attention on others. Remember that giving is an inherent part of receiving.

◆

Chapter 5

The Intelligent Design of Work

"Nothing will work unless you do."

MAYA ANGELOU

POET

Chapter 5

The Intelligent Design of Work

ONE of the most wonderful things to come out of those dark days was the appreciation New Yorkers felt for their protectors. We were grateful for them. Survivors repeated over and over again, "I saw the firemen coming up the stairs and I felt relieved. They were running in as we were running out." Suddenly everyone in the city had a deeper understanding about what these people did for a living each and every day. Most of us have revered firefighters since childhood. But many of us took them for granted until that day. Now that we needed their help, their jobs were more essential than ever.

We began realizing there were many other protectors among us: not just the firefighters, but the police, the First Response teams, EMS workers and the medical community. We saw all of them with renewed appreciation for their life-saving vocations. For the first time in many decades, New Yorkers saw their police force as heroes. The police, who had more commonly been viewed as enemies, were clearly our friends. In the wake of this horror, people acknowledged the status of their police as protectors.

The National Guard was a comforting presence. We were grateful to them for being here. The ironworkers, whom many of us had never thought about before, helped the city tremendously in our crisis. The monumental job of hauling away huge amounts of debris fell into their hands. We read every day about the dedication of the steel and construction workers who helped in the rescues and then in the recovery. Sanitation workers who assist us daily in a very necessary way were often not appreciated before the tragedy. Now they had the overwhelming task of cleaning up the city after this destruction. All of a sudden, we understood their crucial contribution to our lives.

BEING OF SERVICE

The importance of every job was seen in a new light, from the street cleaners, to the corner newspaper salespeople, to those who served us coffee in the morning, to each and every job around us. The tragedy allowed us to see the inherent worth in other people's work that we normally took for granted. We were thankful for each other. We valued the work of one another and saw it for the important contribution it had in the smooth functioning of our city. We considered what our lives would be like without police, firefighters, the medical community, EMS, public transit, construction, sanitation, ironworkers and steelworkers. All of us realized how dependent we were on each other for our comfort and survival.

Wall Street acknowledged publicly and privately the contribution of their blue-collar peers. The traditional lines of separation between them vanished. The Wall Street community was grateful for their continued support and effort, and Wall Streeters began to see their own work in the context of helping others. We had a task in the rebuilding, too. If we did not go back to work and rebuild our industry quickly, the country would suffer further. We personally saw our obligation as something other than the self-serving occupation it had been prior to this event. Now it had a more noble purpose. That was the only way many of us could continue, by believing that our work was of service to others.

Work as a Divine Plan

Two months after the attack, we visited a seventy-three-year old friend of ours in the hospital. The attack had been too stressful for her and we were concerned about a potential heart attack or stroke. As the nurse confidently took her blood and reassured her with comforting words, we sighed in relief. We thought, "Thank God for this nurse. We are so glad she is here." It occurred to us that if this wonderful caregiver did not have to work, she might not be here. If no one had to work, there might not be any nurses at all.

In that moment, we realized the spiritual purpose of work. We thought about the extraordinary importance of the work people did around us since the attack. Without work, our society would not function. Our lives would be unrecognizable. Where would any of us be if we did not have to work? Lying on a beach somewhere? Golfing? Betting at the track? Who would be there to help us if no one had to work? How would our garbage be picked up or the trains run? Who would protect us from harm? How would we be able to survive?

Immediately after the attack, we both thought about folding up our business and buying an old farmhouse somewhere along the Maine coast. The idea of ceasing to work in our business and spending our days reading on the porch or fishing in the sea appealed to our exhausted minds. We asked each other, "Couldn't we just quit and live a less hectic life far away from the threat of terrorism and the grind of Wall Street?" In the shadow of the heroes that surrounded us, we wondered what value our work had, if any, to our community.

As always when we asked a question, we received an answer almost immediately from the mysterious intelligence that guides us. It came in the form of an unexpected phone call from a derivatives trader we had placed at a large firm several years before. "You changed the course of my life," he said. With that call, we realized the purpose of our job in a new way. Every phone call we made had the potential to advance a person's life. We weren't just headhunters; we were *life-changers*. We began to see our business endeavors as spiritual endeavors. We were catalysts in the forward movement of people's lives. We did contribute in a real and positive way to the world around us.

This realization allowed us to see everyone's work as having intrinsic spiritual value. What could be more valuable in the scheme of life than a hard day's work? Each person has an important contribution to make. We depend on each other for our very existence. When we need food in our culture, we walk into a grocery store and purchase it. How many individuals are responsible for that food being there? When we put gas in our car, are we aware of all the individuals who helped make this possible?

The web of connection to each other through our work became crystal clear. Work was the thing that bound us together. It was a spiritual function for each of us. It was important to view our work in terms of how it helped others. We needed to remember to be grateful to the person behind the counter in a store, the person who delivered our mail, as well as everyone else who contributed to our comfort. Work was not the bane of our existence, but an important blessing in our lives. The list of individuals we were dependent on and those who were dependent on us seemed to have no beginning and no end. Through our work, each one of us was a link in the human chain of life.

After the tragedy of September 11, we fully understood the incredible brilliance behind the divine plan of work. We had a spiritual as well as practical obligation to serve each other through our jobs. It was obvious that the value of an individual's work was not based on the amount he or she was paid. The value of the work of the firefighters, who earned in one year what many Wall Streeters earned in one week, could not be disputed. The tragedy broadened our awareness of the importance of each of our jobs. We no longer took for granted the work of others. Work had a spiritual purpose behind it that ensured the functioning of our society in every way. This seemed to be directed by a higher form of intelligence that understood our human selfishness better than we did ourselves. Our need to work forced us to be of service to each other. From the teachers in our schools, to the orderlies in our hospitals, to the CEOs of Fortune 500 companies, all of us had an important role in the continuation of our lives that could not be measured in monetary terms.

◆

Lesson 5

You serve others through the intelligent design of work

"If a man is called to be a street sweeper, he should sweep streets even as Michelangelo painted, or as Beethoven composed music or Shakespeare wrote poetry. He should sweep the streets so well that all the hosts of heaven and earth will pause to say, 'Here lived a great street sweeper who did his job well.'"

MARTIN LUTHER KING, JR.
CIVIL RIGHTS LEADER

You serve others through the intelligent design of work

NURSES, firefighters and First Responders of all kinds are part of what we call the "helping" professions. It is essential to broaden that view by realizing that *every* job is a helping profession. Working makes us part of a sacred covenant. When you are sick, you trust your doctor to give you the correct diagnosis. You count on your lawyer to defend your rights and not mislead you. You expect the individuals who build your house to act honorably. You assume the restaurant you eat in prepares your food under healthy conditions. You count on the pharmacist to supply you with proper medicine. If you expect those you depend on to honor their sacred contract of trust, you must also honor yours. When you accept a job, you may mistakenly believe it is just for yourself. Instead, consider your work for the service it provides to others. All work has the moral and spiritual purpose of honoring the needs of others as well as your own. You make your money and others make theirs by being of service to one another.

The spiritual value of your individual work is related, not to its status in our society, but in the value it has towards the lives of others. Since all jobs have the same basic purpose of directly contributing to the betterment of human life, then all jobs have equal spiritual value. It is only the human ego that convinces us otherwise. Whether you affect one person or millions, you are part of a complicated system of service. You depend on others for fair and reasonable behavior. They also depend on you. For example, the janitor in a company should be respected in the same way the president of a company is due to their equal spiritual contribution. Both jobs are of a nurturing nature. Their spiritual essence derives from their care and concern for the firm. How can anyone perform a job to the best of his ability if he or she is not to be respected for doing it? It is crucial to recognize that if you don't value others, then on a very deep level, you don't value yourself.

We cannot base the spiritual worth of our jobs on monetary compensation. These values are not equal. A job, such as that of a nurse, when performed for its purpose of healing illness and easing discomfort has life itself as its highest value. There is a deeply spiritual connection formed between a nurse and a patient. Even though the compensation for a doctor is much greater, it does not give it more importance. They are both sacred services when performed for the highest good of those involved.

There is great beauty in our work. Work offers us the opportunity to open our hearts to each other. We cherish human life through our jobs. Teachers to students, performers to audiences, waiters to diners, salespeople to buyers, brokers to investors, priests to parishioners, bankers to savers, home-builders to families, mechanics to car-owners, dentists to patients, taxi drivers to fares, barbers to customers and the list goes on. Each of these relationships forms a personal connection.

Through work, we transcend human selfishness and discover our innate human goodness. There is an intelligent design behind work that encourages us to look beyond our own immediate circle of friends and family to the larger world. Work binds us together, obligates us to one another and forces us to be of service to people we don't even know. This is the sacred contract of work.

Through work, we can diminish, damage or destroy others. We hold great power over others in our jobs. However, like firefighters, we can choose to improve the lives of complete strangers. Work is given to us for a higher purpose than we may be able to see. All we need to do is open our eyes to the many lives we touch through our work and recognize the basic spiritual calling in it.

KEY POINTS IN LESSON FIVE

› The spiritual purpose of work is to serve each other.

› Every job is a helping profession.

› All jobs have equal spiritual value.

› There is an intelligent design behind our work that binds us together.

HOW DOES LESSON FIVE MANIFEST IN YOUR PROFESSIONAL LIFE?

EXAMPLE #1

PERSONAL INJURY ATTORNEY

There was a young woman in her late twenties who dreamed of having an important and well-paying job. Her working-class roots had been a deep source of shame for her. She worked behind the counter of a diner, and was also a limo driver, a waitress in a luncheonette and a secretary for a travel agency. She felt all these jobs to be unworthy of her.

To remedy this, she decided to go to law school, sponsored by her parents. It wasn't that she was particularly interested in law; it just seemed the best way out of her circumstances that she could find.

After finishing law school, she worked for a family friend at a personal injury firm. She was excited about the prospect of winning big settlements. But a frantic desire for wealth gave her limited patience in the climb up the ladder. She changed firms often. Every potential client was a dollar sign for her. Whether or not she had prior experience, she assured them she had. Each time she mishandled a case, she claimed it was someone else's fault. Finally, she found herself fired from the fourth law firm in five years.

A cousin, who had long supported her when her parents had refused, felt sorry for her dilemma. He offered her a job as his secretary at a small design firm. This position was a blow to her self-image, so she did not take the new job very seriously. When the cousin wasn't present, instead of working, she spent hours chatting on the phone and reading gossip magazines. She seemed to have little concern or value for her cousin as her employer or for the firm itself, and spoke disparagingly of them to others. She was shocked when her cousin called it quits. She decided her only option was to practice law on her own. To her dismay, she discovered that she had great difficulty attracting clients.

EXAMPLE #2

SENIOR PARTNER, GENERAL PRACTICE LAW FIRM

The life and success of a brilliant trial attorney was the epitome of the American dream. His farming parents had emigrated from Greece before his birth to create more opportunities for their seven children. Throughout his life, he cherished his American heritage by always being the best at everything. He graduated from his high school as the valedictorian and completed his undergraduate degree on a full academic scholarship. When he enlisted in the military in the Second World War, he became the youngest officer in the Army Air Corps. In law school, he finished his degree at night while working full-time to support his aging parents.

He then worked for several years in a top law firm before opening his own firm with a close friend. Theirs was a great partnership: his partner loved to cultivate their clientele on the golf course, and he loved the mental challenge of a courtroom. The only friction in their union was his insistence on devoting half of his time to pro bono work. His expressed goal for retirement was to establish a full-time free legal service for those who couldn't afford quality legal help. For him, law was a noble profession created for the purpose of safeguarding equal rights and opportunity for everyone. To his partner's frustration, he sometimes became more involved in defending the underdog than the high-paying cases that supported their firm. Because of his remarkable talent for litigation, his partner accepted these idiosyncrasies.

One of his most difficult pro bono cases involved an old man who lived on a small estate in New Jersey horse country. The man came to him after being turned down by three other attorneys. As he had no money for even a small retainer, it was hardly worth their time. During his wife's long illness, the eighty-four-year-old man had depleted his assets by using them for medical bills. To generate income, he leased his main house for a fraction of its value to his former caretaker and wife, and moved into the two-room guesthouse on the property. They assured him that if he needed to move back or sell the property, they would leave with reasonable notice. When he wanted to sell the property after his wife's death, the couple refused to leave, citing their contract stipulated a term of ninety-nine years. Somehow during his daily caring for his dying wife, the old man had not noticed this aspect of the contract and relied instead on their verbal assurances.

It was easy to see why no other attorney would touch the case. "A written contract is binding," the lawyers had informed him. Yet the obvious deception by this young couple to sign a ninety-nine-year lease with an ailing old man incensed this lawyer's sense of justice and fair play. He fought hard for his client for seven years, writing brief after brief, appealing his case to each higher court and paying all expenses out of his own pocket. The contract was repeatedly upheld until it reached the highest state appellate court, where it was finally overturned. This case set a legal precedent and was detailed at length in several law journals. Unfortunately, the old man died a few weeks before the final verdict in his favor was rendered. Yet his champion's dedication and compassion reaffirmed his faith in humanity through the last years of life.

APPLYING LESSON FIVE TO YOUR LIFE

Your work affects more lives than you may realize. Your attitudes, thoughts and deeds toward others are part of the human chain of events that connect you. Approaching your work as a spiritual service is a way to change the course of events around you and create a more caring world. In the process, you reap the rewards of your individual contributions to that end.

Tools to Use Your Work as a Service to Others

› View your work as a blessing not a burden.

› Use your work as an opportunity to improve the lives of others.

› Recognize your responsibility to serve others through your work.

Creating a Vision of Our Work as Sacred Through Lesson Five

Choose to see the fundamental spiritual purpose of your work. Understand that you are providing a sacred service to others. Remember that all work is worthy and of equal spiritual value if it is used to improve people's lives. Be responsible to those you affect through your work by making a positive contribution to them.

❖

Chapter 6

The Human Bottom Line

> *"Compassion is not religious business, it is human business, it is not luxury, it is essential for our own peace and mental stability, it is essential for human survival."*
>
> THE DALAI LAMA
> SPIRITUAL LEADER

Chapter 6

The Human Bottom Line

IN the late fall of 2001, the work of the New York City firefighters was extraordinarily difficult. Firehouses were in a
rotation cycle, taking month-long tours digging at the site.
We worried about our friend Mark, who was coughing and
wheezing heavily after digging all day and night. We told him,
"You have to get out of the pit. The air down there is contami-
nated." Mark assured us that leaving Ground Zero was not an
option. "You don't understand," he said. "We can't leave until
we get every firefighter out of there."

The firefighter's code in New York, all over the country
and the world, is the same: "You do not desert your brother.
You go in together, you come out together: dead or alive."
In firefighter training, whether volunteer or paid, this code
was taught from the beginning. An instructor, Tom Butler,
from the Islip New York Volunteer Fire Department and also
a member of New York City's Rescue 4, explained it. He said,
"When a firefighter goes down, you stop what you are doing and you help him first. If he needs air, you give him your
mask. If he is going to die, then you die trying to save him.
You don't leave without your brother." The code is what made
the firefighter's situation after the tragedy all the more poi-

gnant. The guilt the firefighters felt for not being able to save their brothers was enormous.

The continued focus of all of us in New York City on re-building was in large part due to the extraordinary dedication of Mayor Rudy Giuliani. Our beloved mayor had the heart of a firefighter. He mirrored the firefighters and they mirrored him. On the morning of the attack, we were worried about his whereabouts. We waited for the mayor to speak, but no words came. What New Yorkers and the rest of the world did not know was that underneath the rubble of the World Trade Center was Rudy Giuliani with a small group of staff members. The mayor's "secret" downtown command post in the World Trade Center had collapsed with the Towers. Rudy Giuliani crawled out of the rubble the morning of September 11, 2001 to address his city and a hero was born. Despite the loss of friends and colleagues (like all the other First Respond-ers) he showed up to work every day without fail—calm and determined to lead us out of chaos.

Who was Rudy Giuliani before 9/11? As mayor for eight years before the attack, New Yorkers knew him well. No New Yorker had a lukewarm opinion of him; you either loved him or hated him. He either saved the city or ruined it, depending on your view. His tough personality and no-nonsense attitude propelled him from combative New York City district attor-ney to mayor. He garnered support from firefighters before his first election in the early nineties by advocating important fire department improvements. From our personal point of view, he was exactly what the city needed.

Moving to New York for college and footlights in 1979, I saw a different city. In the late seventies and early eighties, women were getting stabbed to death on midtown streets for twenty-dollar gold chains around their necks. Residents were known for "not getting involved" as neighbors were mugged in public view. Taxi drivers were found shot dead in their cabs daily. Criminals put guns to motorists' heads at Park Avenue traffic lights and drove away in their new cars. The subway slasher stalked the commuter trains. Shooter Bernie Goetz exemplified the anxiety of ordinary citizens.

Growing up in a small secluded town in New Jersey's horse country where everyone knew everyone else, the danger and anonymity of New York intrigued me. I remember the first headline I saw in the *New York Post*: "Mayhem Hits the Streets." My parents begged me to come home with each terrifying news report. However, New York was where the action was. Theatre was my first love and New York's theatre was the best in the world. I stayed on and loved it. From my young girl's mind, the city had everything: drama, excitement and adventure. What more could a kid from a sheltered and privileged world want?

Peter, born and bred on East 22nd Street in Brooklyn, remembers a dirty, impoverished, crime-ridden city under Mayor John Lindsay in the 1970s. He lived through race riots, transit strikes and mass looting during the city's blackouts. Lindsay's successor Ed Koch, the quintessential New Yorker of that time, brash and smart, inherited an urban mess and began its revival. He had Giuliani-like qualities in his outspoken boldness. He implemented unpopular but necessary urban renewal programs like limiting rent control. The city's landscape began to slowly improve by the time he left office in 1989. His successor, the soft-spoken Mayor Dinkins, focused on helping the often-overlooked boroughs and improving race relations in a volatile city. Yet under his leadership, the homeless on the streets of Manhattan swelled. A friend from the tony Upper East Side commented, "It looks like Calcutta." The best neighborhoods were teaming with open drug dealing, menacing gangs and crack addicts. Crime levels were out of control. The economy suffered from Wall Street's Black Monday.

New Yorkers did not feel safe or protected. We were scared for our lives.

Enter seasoned crime-fighter, former New York City district attorney, Rudy Giuliani. Within his first two years in office, New York City was transformed: the squatter communities in city parks were eliminated; drug dealers were prosecuted; mandatory sentences were enforced for even the smallest crime; shelters built for the homeless; police officers visible on every corner; rent regulations overhauled; the gangster-run fish market dismantled; and tax incentives created for developers. New York took on new life. In a few short years, New York went from one of America's most dangerous cities to one of the safest. Whatever complaint anyone had about Giuliani as mayor, no one can deny the safe and affluent city of today is a result of his tenure. We saw it with our own eyes. His strength and courage served New York well, before and after the attack. We needed him.

Two months after the attack, to save the city money Mayor Giuliani tried to reduce the number of firefighters digging at the site. In response, firefighters descended on Ground Zero as an angry mob. The November 6, 2001 *New York Times* reported, "500 firefighters and fire officers demonstrated their anger over the city's decision to reduce the number of fire personnel at Ground Zero." For the firefighters, this tragedy could not be reduced to dollars and cents. To them, there was much more at stake. Still reeling from the loss of their brothers, they had to honor the firefighter's code. They could not leave until they got the last man out even if he was at the bottom of 100 stories of debris. As mayor, however, Giuliani had the city's finances to consider. Yet in solidarity with his firefighters, he understood there was much more than money at stake. There was honor, love and most important of all, peace of mind. Mayor Giuliani felt the firefighters' pain deep in his soul. He worked out a compromise that the city could afford and the firefighters could accept. He understood that the human beings involved were as important as the numbers of his budget.

SURVIVAL OF THE FITTEST

Unfortunately as fate would have it, when New York needed him most, Giuliani fulfilled his two-term limit. He and his constituents wanted him to continue as mayor into the following year, but a referendum was shot down by the newly elected mayor, Mike Bloomberg. The new mayor, with no prior political experience, had been elected primarily on the endorsement of Rudy Giuliani. Few knew Mike Bloomberg when he took office in January 2002. Low-key and seemingly detached, Mayor Bloomberg lacked the emotional connection Giuliani had with the city. During his first years in office, most New Yorkers thought him a cold, heartless businessman who valued numbers, not people.

It took three years for people to realize that he was the kind of billionaire that made being rich a noble calling. A deeply principled man, he was intent on devoting his considerable business expertise to curing the ills of the city's management. News reports quoted him as saying, "I will do what I think is right." He clearly understood his work as a service to others. He took one dollar as his salary and personally donated millions of dollars to city causes. He was a passionate reformer for New York City's ailing school system and dedicated himself to ensure that every child received a quality education. Unlike other individuals who might have used this position for personal gain, Bloomberg's goal seemed to be to genuinely improve his native city.

A brilliant businessman, the new mayor had created his vast fortune as an information service provider catering to Wall Street. He was committed to saving the city from economic disaster. To this end, he used his business acumen to eliminate spending wastes wherever he could. He enraged residents by laying off thousands of city workers, including teachers, reducing garbage pickups, eliminating basic programs like recycling, and raising property taxes 18% in the midst of a deep recession. As business managers ourselves in post-9/11 New York, we understood drastic actions were needed to keep the city afloat. The city was on the verge of economic collapse. Traditional cost cutting might just save it. We were doing the same thing in our firm, eliminating any unnecessary expense, letting go of contract workers and consultants, taking no salary for ourselves, reducing our remaining employees' salaries and paring down our overhead to weather the financial storms ahead. This was more than an ordinary recession. In New York throughout 2002 and much of 2003, it was closer to an economic depression. Business methodology dictates, "Slash costs wherever possible," and we did. However, we kept our most valued employees on the payroll despite the loss of revenue that year, by financing this with personal funds. People were the foundation of our business. They were as vital to the future of the firm as we were ourselves. As we suffered the fallout of this tragedy together, we understood it was about more than money: our survival through this catastrophe depended on each other.

Despite the economic reality of reduced spending, in the spring of 2003, it came as a shock to New Yorkers when the new mayor decided to close neighborhood firehouses. This was a measure of extreme proportions for most residents and firefighters. Cost cutting was one thing; reducing the number of firehouses after they played such a critical role in the city's recovery was entirely different. People viewed this action as inhumane both to the firefighters and the neighborhoods that lost their protection. In response to the mayor's threat to close down fourteen firehouses throughout the city, one firefighter quipped, "He's just a businessman." However, the city was not just a business to the firefighters—it was home to several million people to whom they were responsible. The oath of a New York City firefighter is "to protect the life and property of the city of New York." In a *New York Daily News* article on April 9, 2003, Stephen Cassidy, the president of the Uniformed Firefighters Association, explained that closing firehouses would jeopardize people's safety and could "result in deaths to civilians and firefighters." However, to the mayor, the city was the employer of hundreds of thousands of workers and most definitely a business. He was responsible for protecting the city's finances as well as its people.

The closeness between Wall Street and the FDNY diminished after the tragedy as the age-old conflict between business and their protectors began again. A professional moneyman, the mayor mirrored the actions of his investment-banker counterparts and cut the fat wherever he could with his no-frills policy. This included ultimately closing six firehouses he deemed "unnecessary." Yet after 9/11, few New Yorkers thought of any city firehouse as excess fat or frills. In a letter to the editor in a local newspaper, a bystander expressed this view: "It would be a grave injustice to the memory of the 343 firefighters who lost their lives on 9/11, as well as to the sense of security of every New Yorker, to proceed with closing even one firehouse." Yet to the mayor, it was a clear-cut business decision. He needed to reduce costs for the sake of the city's finances wherever possible. Yet the residents' fragile sense of security was on the line.

Money Talks

The mayor was doing a great job of balancing an out-of-control financial situation. He successfully pulled New York City's budget out of the red and into the black. The wisdom of conventional business dictated that these harsh methods were necessary. It was a simple, cut-and-dry economic decision. Anything expendable, including underused firehouses, had to be eliminated in order for the city to survive financially. The mayor assured the communities affected that his decision was nothing personal. It was just business. But for the residents in those communities it was indeed very personal.

In justifying the closing of a firehouse in Queens, New York, the mayor argued that the firehouse was not essential since that neighborhood could share fire services with an adjacent neighborhood. Upon the advice of experts and the history of activity in this firehouse, he determined that this closing would pose little threat to the safety of the city's people. The firefighters responded to his argument with an example of a family of four whose lives had been saved that very week, within minutes of their death. According to the *New York Daily News* on February 21, 2003, firefighters claimed that the additional minutes it would have taken to reach these victims from another firehouse would have cost them their lives. This issue highlighted the contrast between capitalism of the old school versus capitalism with a conscience: strictly adhering to the bottom line versus placing a value on the adverse affects on human lives. Is it reasonable to close a firehouse to save money if there is a possibility of the loss of even one life? Or put another way, do we sacrifice one or more lives for economic gain?

The mayor's viewpoint was the result of an old and accepted belief system: "money talks." In traditional business, it is dollars and cents; there is little room for sentiment. This view is absolutely accurate if money is the *only* bottom line. According to the principles of traditional capitalism, which place no limits on cost cutting, the mayor made all the right decisions. The proof lay in the fact that he managed to avoid bankruptcy for the city, and no experienced money manager would have done anything differently. However, in the wake of the sacrifice made by these individuals in one of the worst disasters ever to occur on American soil, closing New York City firehouses to save the city money seemed grossly inappropriate. How could we repay our saviors by reducing firefighting services and possibly risking more people's lives?

In the last century, our society witnessed the abolition of child labor, the creation of worker unions and the humanizing of labor laws. Wasn't it time to humanize the bottom line in our business affairs? If we take the perspective of spiritual capitalism, an unspoken agreement was being violated. A leader of any kind serves his or her public, whether it is a client, customer or constituent. Therefore dismissing the needs of the public you cater to is a grave misjudgment of your duty as a service provider. The public view is that officials owe at least a hearing to constituent needs. Part of what the mayor had to learn in his first term was how to humanize his stance and unlearn standard business indifference in the process.

In strict economic terms, Giuliani's compromise at Ground Zero may have been unwise, but he found an economic middle ground. Instead of slashing 60% of the workforce, he rotated worker shifts to allow all the firefighters to be at Ground Zero part of the time. In the process he revealed himself as a practical *and* visionary leader. He recognized the human aspect of the situation, thereby quelling a growing mutiny among his employees. In the end he served both—the economic and human bottom lines—thus winning the hearts and minds of his workers and public while insuring their continued support.

In contrast, Bloomberg in his new role of public servant adhered to customary CEO practices by cutting costs across the board. He was viewed by many to be harsh and inhumane. Was he wrong? No, not by the standards of traditional capitalism. Cold hard cash was his master, and he served his master well. Yet in human terms, he failed to fully serve his public by refusing to incorporate their needs into the bottom line.

A Numbers Game

Mayor Bloomberg has proven that on many levels he is a responsible and honorable manager. Forgoing his own salary, he staved off an economic collapse of colossal proportions. His business management style and expertise worked wonders for our wounded city, and we are flourishing again. Wall Street is booming. Real estate values are soaring ever higher. The new mayor has improved upon Giuliani's legacy by creating one of the best police forces in the world. He responds immediately to any confirmed or unconfirmed terrorist threat. Crime is down. Racial tensions are low. Tourism and the local economy are on the upswing. In his recent election, he easily won another term. In so many ways New Yorkers owe him a debt of gratitude for his dedication to our city's survival. We feel safe again.

Yet despite his other successes, the shuttered New York City firehouses lurk in the minds of local residents. This action cost him much devotion as it left the impression of him as a coldhearted businessman. Accepting that Mayor Bloomberg is a decent and ethical person, we cannot attribute his detachment to lack of character. It is the simple determination of a self-made billionaire who believes that cash is king. Many *good* people in business appear heartless when it comes to numbers.

We bring this up not to vilify a mayor that we ourselves support. We use this example only to highlight a common mistake business managers make when they ignore the human cost in the bottom line. Unfortunately, managers are trained that way. Standard operating procedure is to place the greatest value on numbers not people. Does a money manager have the responsibility to maximize profits and minimize spending? Absolutely—yet like any other enlightened businessperson, he or she also has a social responsibility to the public he serves.

Traditional capitalism often does not take individual people into account. In the closing of the firehouses, local news reports claimed the city saved $8 million. Firefighter Edward Cammon, who worked for Engine 36 on 125th Street in Harlem for forty years, summed this point up by stating, "As far as the city's concerned, we're talking pocket change, and you equate that with human life?" Perhaps we can help modern managers understand that business is not *only* about numbers anymore, that human lives do carry value in the equation. In our twenty-first century we need to combine self-interest with world interest if we are to be functioning capitalists with a conscience.

TURNING A DEAF EAR

Businesses are frequently in decision-making positions comparable to those faced by New York City's mayors. Commonly, managers conclude that savings are needed regardless of who is adversely affected. Often there is no other alternative and decisions like these appear harsh, but they are necessary. Equally often, however, there are viable options available if we stretch our business acumen. We can develop ways to think out of the box and use our creative resources to devise less painful solutions. First we must believe that preserving the welfare of individuals in our pursuit of profit is a desirable goal. Then we must incorporate humane business practices in our focus on the bottom line. Business often believes it does not owe the public an explanation of how it profits; it feels no attachment to customers. The public reacts to this attitude with frustration and rage, and their protests normally fall on deaf ears. In strict legal terms, managers only have a duty to the bottom line. Many managers think if they profit, they are serving their purpose. The human element is a non-issue.

As businesspeople, we sympathized with oil company executives who sat before a United States Senate committee in late 2005. The five CEOs were not queried on illegal activities, but on legal and financially responsible ones. By maximizing profits for their shareholders, they were vilified as evil monsters out to destroy the little guy. The CEOs exploded with indignation when asked to defend upholding their fiduciary duty.

At the same time we felt sympathy for those whose incomes were already stretched to the max, agonizing over a 30% hike in gas prices. The impropriety of the rate increase lay in the amount as well as the timing, having occurred during Hurricane Katrina, a national tragedy of monumental proportions. As the nation jumped to help the victims in their struggle for survival, the oil companies chose that moment to spike rates at the pump. Oil companies claimed they were protecting their assets; to the majority of the nation, they appeared to be cold-blooded extortionists.

Where was the middle ground here? The Gang of Five's seeming indifference to humanity enraged people. As the oil magnates exercised their basic American right to free enterprise, the public demanded a limit on such harsh capitalism. The moguls failed to recognize that modern capitalism is being called to include an element of compassion in its practice. Exploiting a human tragedy to profit seems ugly even to traditional capitalists. The oil execs' belligerence made them appear callous and greedy, yet they stuck to their profit-at-any-cost guns and insisted they answer to no one other than shareholders. The public service aspect of their product, however, forces oil companies to adjust profit margins to public needs. Yes, they had a record quarter in profits and wanted to protect those earnings. Yet their self-serving actions cost them a steep price in public opinion. Not surprisingly, pump prices returned to pre-disaster levels quickly in response to public outrage.

A member of the House of Representatives declared, "Oil companies owe the American people an explanation" for their actions. We wondered how a company owes the public an explanation for being fiscally responsible to its shareholders. This extraordinary statement underlines a basic conflict between the fiduciary duty of a corporation to increase profits for shareholders and the public who increasingly believe that corporations must answer to them as well. The question on the table with oil company profits is, do corporations have a duty to the community that supports them as well as to their profits? The answer in modern society is, increasingly, yes.

People are a Dime a Dozen

Business understands how crucial its image is to the modern company's bottom line. Wal-Mart is routinely accused by critics of employing Carnegie-like actions toward their employees. (Andrew Carnegie was a Gilded Age industrialist, infamous for his poor treatment of employees: he purposely underpaid steelworkers to insure their financial servitude, and at the threat of a strike, he told his large workforce to go ahead and strike as they were easily replaced.) In response to a threat of unionization at a Canadian branch, rather than offer workers better pay or benefits, the cheap-goods giant Wal-Mart closed shop and moved to another location. "People are a dime a dozen," one worker observed.

Although Wal-Mart is highly profitable, they manage a balancing act with public opinion. In recent years, the company has been cited in news reports for seemingly abusive worker policies. An inner office directive from a top company executive in the fall of 2005 detailed a new company policy to hire only fit and healthy workers and discourage long-term employment to save on healthcare and pension costs. The memo released to the press anonymously added fuel to the already worker-hostile image held by many observers. Wal-Mart executives quickly launched a publicity campaign to combat their growing negative image. These efforts reveal the company's fear that customers will become so repulsed by this behavior that they will boycott their cheap products. This further proves that when it comes to money, morality and conscience do matter to the general public.

It is easy to profit off the backs of others. Work an employee hard, pay them a poverty wage with little or no benefits, and slice them from the books when they are no longer useful. Where is the managerial talent in this approach? This basic survival-of-the-fittest profiteering requires no imagination or innovation. Yet very often, despite many other options, these practices are called "good management."

On the other hand, the enormously profitable tech giant, Microsoft, is one of the most sought-after employers. Stock options, stellar health insurance and a comfortable working environment are just a few of the employee perks. Powerhouses Google and Starbucks are equally desirable employers. Their success seems to contradict the old capitalist belief that worker exploitation is necessary to profit. Using intellect and creative energy to create profit while valuing the workforce, these companies serve as role models of a new concept of "good" management.

A Source of Trouble

We would be remiss if we didn't include outsourcing and offshoring in our examination of the human cost in business. Many honorable economists insist that outsourcing (using foreign labor via fiber-optic technology) and offshoring (moving U.S. factories to foreign soil) are important steps for our global economy. Companies often use these cost-saving methods to remain "competitive." In the 1980s, President Reagan assured anxious Americans that manufacturing jobs going offshore would be replaced with service jobs. Twenty years later service jobs are moving offshore. What will replace them? Where are the solutions for companies to keep costs down with overseas labor and yet create new opportunities for American workers?

Retired Federal Reserve Chairman Alan Greenspan and the billionaire fund manager Warren Buffett insist these practices will benefit the U.S. in the long term. We don't know for sure, and brilliant business minds that they are, they can't be certain either. The two men are highly respected throughout the business world for their personal integrity, so we want to believe them. But none of us have a crystal ball.

Both sides of the outsourcing/offshoring spectrum have merit, hence the controversy of the issue. There is no simple answer. Change is as basic an element in business as in any other area of life. If we are to flourish and survive we must adapt as quickly as possible. Yet even if we accept the nebulous argument that it will all turn out for the best, what about the shorter term? How will it be for those affected now? There is something unduly cruel about forcing long-term employees to train their foreign replacements. Even more questionable is a corporation who uses offshoring to impoverish an entire community to increase profits or inflate their own executives' earnings, especially when there might have been another way.

Corporations seem to be following the crowd. Some executives are aware of how inhumane the public views this practice to be. "It's the absence of a public policy that tells me what to do," former Intel CEO Andrew Grove stated. "I have no choice as a corporate manager, nor do my colleagues... [to make decisions] that very often involve moves of jobs into other countries."

A January 2006 *BusinessWeek* article cites examples of companies that hired 2,000 Indian workers, each at one-tenth the cost of the 100 American workers they employ. Judging from this, new jobs seem to be trickling down in U.S. corporations to American workers about 5% of the time. Outsourcing companies are indeed growing, but on the *other* side of our shores.

These practices simplify the hiring and firing process considerably. When we hire workers in these countries there are no Social Security, disability, workers' compensation, Unemployment Insurance or minimum wages to pay. But wait... weren't these laws created to protect the American worker? These facts make the outrage of some Americans in response to outsourcing understandable. Just because it is legal to outsource and offshore *without* replenishing the system doesn't make it right. Something is missing here—*responsibility.*

As business maverick John D. Rockefeller said, "The world owes no man a living but it owes every man an opportunity to make a living." The business community cannot turn a blind eye to a job deficit that it is helping to create. Profitable companies that have a financial stake in outsourcing and offshoring have a moral responsibility to those people they dismiss—that is if they truly care about our nation's economic and social future.

BACK TO BUSINESS

Competitive cost cutting, however, is essential to a company's survival. In our new economic world, business often cannot compete on an equal playing field if it doesn't move production or support work overseas. As experienced businesspeople who prize our free enterprise system, we sympathize with managers who wrestle with these tough decisions. Business is about creating profits, staying afloat and keeping the competitive edge.

Yet, instead of putting our heads in the sand or offering up smoke screens that attempt to disguise pure profit-seeking as innovation, we need to acknowledge there is a growing problem before we can resolve it. A McKinsey poll predicts that 4.1 million blue-collar and white-collar jobs will go offshore by 2008. A University of California, Berkeley study estimates the job losses will number closer to 14 million for U.S. workers by 2010. No matter which estimate is correct, the fact remains there is an ever-widening hole in our "onshore" labor market.

Outsourcing the middle class of America could not possibly be good for our national bottom line. A large part of the engine of our economy depends on the consumer middle class. Without them our "affluent society" would not exist. Therefore this problem directly affects us all. In July 2005, *Fortune* magazine journalist Geoffrey Colvin wrote, "The stakes are mammoth: Respectable analysts believe it's possible—not certain, but possible—that the U.S. standard of living, after decades of steady ascent, could stall or even begin to decline."

One of the questions often posed to support outsourcing is, "Don't you want India and China to do well?" The implication here is that outsourcing is a humanitarian act. We always respond, "Yes, absolutely. We wish for them all the blessings we wish for ourselves." Yet what is our first obligation? You want your neighbors down the street to do well, but would it be "right" if you neglected your own children to take care of theirs? Don't we have a responsibility first to our own families and then to others? Certainly we owe our own citizens economic protection also.

So, what is a *good* CEO supposed to do? Well... *something*. Doing nothing is not a responsible option. David Neeleman, CEO of Jet Blue Airways, uses "home sourcing" as an alternative to outsourcing for his company. He hires stay-at-home moms at $8.25 an hour to field customer-service calls from the comfort of their homes. Former COO and president of Oracle Corp. Ray Lane suggests, "Take some of your expected profits from offshoring and make your severance packages higher or retrain the employees in known growth industries." To offset some of its U.S. job losses, IBM established a retraining fund of $25 million for U.S. workers whose current positions are being outsourced to India, Pakistan and China.

There are many positive outcomes for our economy and global unity to be derived from offshoring and outsourcing. Bringing the world together through commerce can be beneficial for all countries involved. Hopefully, the enormous cost savings for companies can encourage expansion on our own shores as well. Yet the current status quo of outsourcing and offshoring with no regulation or limit is like a bloodletting— only no one is applying pressure to the wound. Ronil Hira, an assistant professor of public policy at the Rochester Institute of Technology and chair of the workforce policy committee at the Institute of Electrical and Electronics Engineers states, "I'm not against offshoring. I hope that this could be something that transforms and brings lots of people into the modern world. That's within our national interest, but at the same time, I don't think the way it's being done is responsible."

We urgently need to find a fair and balanced solution for both business and labor. Globalization is here to stay, but we can lessen the growing pains by considering the cost to human beings. Perhaps we can create a think tank of business managers, corporate executives, economists, analysts, scholars, labor organizers, workers and lawmakers and use this combined brain power to devise more equitable solutions. Or perhaps each CEO will consider a more humane approach before shoving workers out the door. In his book, *The World is Flat*, Tom Friedman reminds us, "The great challenge for our time will be to absorb these changes in ways that do not overwhelm people but also do not leave them behind."

Our Brother's Keeper

Naturally, we need to maximize profit. But how do we answer for our compromised humanity to the sacrificed worker? Howard Stringer, the new CEO of the giant electronics manufacturer Sony, questions the "American business model of ruthlessness and viciousness" in slashing the workforce without reasonable consideration of their needs. As the former CEO of CBS News, he refused to lay off his workers with the traditional written memo. Instead he faced each downsized individual personally as a gesture of basic respect. He is currently facing large layoffs at Sony, but insists he will treat the jobless with dignity.

Montreal business mogul, J-Robert Ouimet, the chairman and CEO of Holding O.C.B. Inc. and Ouimet-Tomasso, Inc., a highly successful food-processing company in Canada, also emphasizes the value of human dignity when firing employees. Worker "layoffs" at Ouimet-Tomasso are handled much differently than other firms. The firing manager is required to meet with each terminated employee for "coffee or lunch" over the course of the following months to understand the personal impact of his or her actions. This extraordinary humanitarian gesture holds management directly accountable for its business decisions. At Ouimet-Tomasso, Inc. and Holding O.C.B. Inc., business is understood to be "personal" for everyone at the firm from top management down. CEO Ouimet explains his unusual management style: "As managers, we must carry in our hearts the colossal importance of what impact our management will have on employees." Powerful CEOs Ouimet and Stringer view economic indifference as irresponsible managing in the new millennium.

Put Your Money Where Your Mouth Is

Who are we in business? Are we the robber barons of yesteryear, glibly walking over weaker individuals to reach ever-greater profits? Are we vicious profiteers ready to destroy everything and everyone in our path? Or are we ethical people who care about how our behavior affects others? We must find the balance between our personal morality and our business prowess.

We are compassionate people in America. Most of us want to do the right thing. Put your money where your mouth is and be part of the solution not the problem. Public sentiment equates the heartless "every man for himself" view in business with extortion. There seems to be a call for a middle ground. Something more evolved than our Gilded Age predecessors—a balance to be struck between profit at any cost and public concern. No matter what doctrinaire, old school capitalists say, the general public believes social responsibility is an obligatory part of modern business operating procedure.

It's War

Very often in modern business we approach making money like we are going to war. "It's us or them," we think in our quest for profits. "Take no prisoners. Casualties are unfortunate but necessary." These views often color employee layoffs. The workers we leave behind are simply civilian casualties. Just as in war, we detach ourselves from the suffering of others. We cannot pause to think of the carnage we create or our own lives will be vulnerable. We become indifferent as we focus on our cause: the bottom line. The ends justify the means and we cannot be held accountable in our struggle for survival. Or can we? Do the ends ever truly justify the means?

War is a last resort. Great military leaders understand this, and great business leaders should too. In war, the military knows there will be huge loss and destruction of life; in business, we can destroy lives too. Do we simply turn away, refusing to recognize the damage we inflict? Or do we act responsibly to our civilian population and include humanity in the equation? How are we going to win the hearts and minds of the people if we are causing them harm?

In reality, business is *not* war. Its purpose is to replenish, not to destroy or conquer. It exists to *create* products, services and wealth that contribute to human well-being. The time has come to drop our war-like mentality in business, to instead enhance our world, not diminish it. In doing so, we generate a lasting prosperity of the soul as well as the mind.

♦

Lesson 6

Calculate the human cost into the bottom line

"One life on this planet is no more valuable than the next."

MELINDA GATES

BILLIONAIRE, PHILANTHROPIST

Lesson 6

Calculate the human cost into the bottom line

WE have lost touch with our human side in business. A little more than a century ago, business moved from small community endeavors to nationwide industries, and with that expansion went the personal connection. Small businesses ordinarily cannot afford to be cutthroat, as they depend on face-to-face relationships. Big business believes itself removed from this reality. They can't see the faces of those they alienate or destroy. Therefore they are not forced to reconcile themselves with their actions.

As industry expands globally, business is even less personal than before. Just because we cannot see the faces of those we do business with does not mean they are not there. If we want to evolve intellectually and socially as much as we are economically, we must include the human cost in the bottom line, and find solutions that serve humanity as well as our profit margin.

According to Webster's Dictionary, *humane* is defined as "marked by compassion, sympathy or consideration." How do we define *business*? Webster defines business as "a purposeful activity engaged as a means of livelihood." If we merge these two meanings the resulting definition of *humane business* is "a purposeful human activity as a means of livelihood marked by compassion, sympathy or consideration for others."

If professional firefighters acted with the same indifference in their work as we do in business, we would find this unforgivable. Firefighters however, like nurses, doctors and other people in the helping professions, see their duty to human life as priority. They know they must make a living and profit in the process. Yet without life-preserving qualities, their work loses its value. Medical professionals who care for patients by rote with obvious lack of concern are seen as callous and dehumanizing. We demand compassion along with their expertise. A doctor who possesses sensitivity to patients is highly sought after. A firefighter captures our heart because of his dedication to our welfare in the ordinary course of making a living. All helping professions are held to high expectations that we are not held to in the pursuit of profit.

The purpose of business is not to support the needs of individuals unconditionally—a healthy sense of detachment is necessary in business to respond rationally—nor is it *only* about profit. Somewhere in between profit at any cost and curing society's ills is the new business model: balancing the need of business to maximize profits with the needs of the community it serves. Cost cutting when it negatively impacts human lives should be the *last* resort, not the first. Very often this is the first and only response and other solutions are not even considered.

Our business decisions affect people's lives directly. Therefore it is not only about economic profit and loss, but also human profit and loss. Capitalism must include the human factor in its calculations. We have unpopular and unpleasant decisions to make in our business lives that are necessary for our continued economic survival. We cannot please everyone and never will. The point is to develop a conscience in business, a human conscience that uses the same standards of right and wrong as we do in our personal lives.

Making as much money as possible is our goal. But doing this with a sense of humanity is our challenge. Some of the brightest minds in our society are part of the business community. Can we use our intellects to create a balance between our profit seeking and our social conscience? We know we can profit with the ruthless indifference of our Gilded Age ancestors. The new rules, though, demand we find a way to profit combining our creative, intellectual *and* ethical resources. Our actions are not a result of some indifferent entity known as the "corporation," the "shareholder" or "profits." We, human beings, execute these actions.

As modern capitalists, will we always put money ahead of our humanity? Traditional capitalism that values only the economic bottom line (capitalism without a conscience) is no longer adequate in our enlightened society. It must be replaced with something new—a spiritual capitalism that holds life itself as the ultimate bottom line.

KEY POINTS IN LESSON SIX

› Business has a responsibility to those it affects.

› Capitalism must include the human factor in its calculations.

› The ultimate bottom line is life itself.

How Does Lesson Six Manifest in Your Business Life?

Example #1

Large Appliance Manufacturing Company

An electrical-appliance manufacturing company found it-self at a competitive disadvantage in its projected market share. The solution, according to the firm's top management, was to move their factory to an offshore location that would provide substantially cheaper labor and production costs. This made good business sense.

Problems began when the firm announced the planned layoffs of a few thousand people. This accounted for one-third of the population of the small community that had supported the firm for over 100 years. Company executives felt that they had little obligation to their employees beyond the moment. Management's priority was to maximize profits for their company and themselves. The bottom line claimed their allegiance.

The workers, however, held a different view. They gave their all to the company and assumed that the company would give the same in return. The town's leaders quickly jumped in to help strike a balance between the workers and management. They understood that if the company could not continue to profit, it would have no choice but to move production elsewhere. Their strategy was to hire various business experts to find ways to eliminate the company's es-timated losses. The group of engineers, labor officials and financial advisors put together a cost-cutting program that would recover $74 million of the company's potential loss factor. The remaining $7 million would have to be borne by the firm in order to keep thousands of people employed. The chairman of the firm politely declined this offer. He stated, "Economics, not emotions, will be the determining factor."

Example #2

Warehouse Retailer

This remarkable Fortune 500 company achieved a feat many thought impossible: it balanced the needs of employees, managers, customers and shareholders alike. The maverick CEO builds market share in a refreshing way—by offering customers quality and value without exploiting the workforce. Hourly workers are paid more than 40% over competitors, and are supplied with benefits that are unheard of in the industry. Employees pay only 8% for top-quality health and dental insurance and receive hefty 401K contributions from the corporation. Part-time employees are offered insurance after six months on the job. Some 10% of workers are union members. Even union representatives glow about the retailer, claiming they forged "the best agreement" in the industry. The chief executive insists his company must pay employees better than others to create worker loyalty. He has proven that happy employees equal low levels of turnover and employee theft.

To customers, the CEO is equally generous. The company's mark-up is limited to 15% instead of the industry standard of 25%-50%. His purpose in doing this is to develop a loyal customer base. He believes his socially conscious clientele does not want to save money at the expense of workers. Therefore, he limits his profit margins to keep both worker and customer happy.

The CEO pays himself $558,000 in salary and depends on personal profits from rising stock value. He declares that paying employers 100 times or more than the average worker is "wrong." Stock prices have increased steadily by

10% in the past year alone, surpassing the company's direct competitor. The company's ranking has risen higher on the Fortune 500 list and enjoys 50% market share.

The secret competitive edge at this firm seems to be to treat workers and customers fairly and profits will follow. However, the top manager claims this is not about altruism. It is just good business.

APPLYING LESSON SIX TO YOUR LIFE

We carry the pain of everyone we have ever hurt within us. Each time we harm another it is imprinted on our souls. The same holds for our good deeds. These are also imprinted on our souls. When we put the needs of others at the same value as our own, we create a new soul history for ourselves. Including humanity in our business affairs is as healing for us as it is for our world.

TOOLS FOR INCLUDING HUMANITY IN YOUR BUSINESS AFFAIRS

›   Consider all options before negatively affecting people's lives.

›   Compensate or retool displaced workers in a fair and reasonable manner.

›   Honor the human dignity of your workforce.

CREATING A VISION OF HUMANE CAPITALISM

Recognize everyone you meet as a powerful manifestation of the divine source. Honor the divine in them, as you hope they honor the divine in you. Wish for them what you wish for yourself by remembering that you are in each other's lives for a spiritual purpose beyond what you can see. Recognize that humane profit seeking is not a frivolous ideal in today's enlightened world, but an obligation for responsible business.

◆

Chapter 7

An Absence of Trust

> *"Our system works fundamentally on trust and individual fair dealing. We need only look around today's world to realize how valuable these traits are and the consequences of their absence. While we have achieved much as a nation in this regard, more remains to be done."*

ALAN GREENSPAN
U.S. FEDERAL RESERVE CHAIRMAN

THE attack on our financial community on 9/11 was no co-incidence. It was a purposeful assault directed squarely at the heart of Wall Street. When these militants attacked the Towers, the ultimate symbols of American financial supremacy, they perceived American capitalism as the cause of their suffering. Our wealth and success were their enemies. The attack was as much about hatred for our money as it was about politics, religion or vengeance. They felt powerless to our economic prowess. Their goal was clear—to kick us right below the money belt. No matter how distorted or hypocritical their view, no matter that they should have looked in their own backyards first; this tragedy highlights the fact that money and business are held responsible for much of the human suffering in the world.

It wasn't enough that we suffered this cruel judgment from strangers. The nation stood together in grief only to witness the attack on our economic system by our own American business leaders. The phantom planes of Enron hit the Towers of our trusting hearts within three months of the tragedy. It began with the company's bankruptcy and spiraled out of control from there. The books were opened and huge frauds were revealed as part of a conspiracy with the respected accounting firm, Arthur Anderson. Its creditors included most of Wall Street and businesses began running for their lives. Six months later, the details of WorldCom's deception exploded. One attack on our nation's economy followed another—but these were not strangers from far-off lands—these were our very own.

To add salt to the wounds was the revelation of a fraudulent energy crisis created by Enron traders in early 2001. Enron's 1998 Annual Report stated, "We treat others as we would like to be treated ourselves. We do not tolerate abusive or disrespectful treatment. Ruthlessness, callousness and arrogance don't belong here." Enron, who did "not tolerate abusive" behavior, turned off the lights in the State of California in order to extort higher profits. Why does an energy company need a trading floor anyway? Isn't this an obvious conflict of interest, ripe for exploitation? On September 17, 2002, just one year after the terrorist attack, *CBS Evening News* reported the California energy crisis was "a sham." As we recovered from the heavy blows of foreign enemies, we also suffered from this economic terrorism on our own shores.

The Enemy of the People

The scandals have not ceased in the five years since the attack. A series of purposeful disasters rocked our business world even further, as the corporate and Wall Street scandals unfolded. Business seems to be the target. On the heels of the fantasy 1990s, the easy fortune we believed real disappeared as quickly as it appeared. In the aftermath of 9/11 and the years that followed, we see how much of our economy is based on intangibles such as faith and trust—faith in our capitalistic system and trust in our business leaders. Suddenly, with each new headline, the faith that we took for granted is challenged at its deepest level. We no longer know whom or what to trust. For our business community, the shock from these attacks is that we are finally being held responsible for our part in creating the suffering around us.

Although traditional business never thought this way, we clearly see the backlash of unbridled avarice in our economy through the scandals of the past few years. All businesses become suspect when a handful of corporations function in an economic vacuum. Those in business who bent the rules for years with questionable scams damaged the entire market by their own behavior.

Industry after industry has lost consumer confidence. A well-known insurance company, State Farm, bills itself as a "good neighbor." In September 2005, the good neighbor's poor treatment of policy holders and former employees forced the company to pay $20 million in damages. The profitable pharmaceutical company, Merck, advertises itself as a business "where patients come first." The company used excerpts from Martin Luther King's speech on racial equality and freedom, "I have a dream," to advertise its deadly drug Vioxx. Since the recall of this pain reliever, a common perception of the company is, ironically, "profits come first."

The insurance company AIG has been under fire for corporate improprieties. The CEO and long-time chairman, Hank Greenberg, was forced to step down under a legal investigation. He is accused personally of stock manipulations and questionable accounting practices going back fourteen years. Under his leadership, AIG has admitted to inflating earnings to the tune of $2.7 billion. In the ultimate irony, Greenberg wrote to shareholders in 2003: "The whole country is paying a price for the gross misdeeds of relatively few executives who shirked their responsibility to create value for all of their corporate constituencies—shareholders, customers and employees—and abused the system to create wealth for themselves

---

and their close associates. It is unfortunate that the misbehavior of a few companies and their executives could have a negative impact on so many." Whether Greenberg himself is responsible for these acts or his staff has not been definitively established. However, he describes the "gross misdeeds" that he himself is accused of as "abuse." His letter reveals that he understands how damaging this behavior is to public interests.

As we travel the country, we are astounded to hear that most Americans have completely lost faith in business. Business is viewed as the neighborhood bully of modern society. It beats us up and gets away with it. We are scared of it, awed by it, repulsed by it, enraged by it. It does not comfort us or value us. We are pawns in its gigantic chess game for profit. Many people feel that business has too often deceived us for its own gain only to abandon us in the end. Business has become the enemy of the people. It is hated and reviled. It will rape and pillage us—not serve us. These are the common sentiments we hear from ordinary Americans.

RENEWING FAITH

In direct contrast to the common view of business, is the esteem with which we hold firefighters. We trust them with our hearts and our lives. They will never let us down. We count on them to protect us. We see them as our saviors. What moved us so deeply during the attack on our nation was their uncomplaining dedication to our welfare. Heartbroken and devastated as they were, they still functioned with honor and integrity. Yet this is what a firefighter does every day—out of the limelight. They take an oath to protect people. Perhaps we should take an oath in business—to protect our customers and stand by our product or service. Could you imagine a firefighter throwing a victim a rope that was not really there? This is what we do when we falsify our product or service.

The mistrust that firefighters themselves have for business was evident when Peter became a volunteer in our community. As he pulled up to the firehouse in his sporty BMW to join the department, the firefighters viewed him with suspicion. One lieutenant later told him, "I thought, why would a millionaire businessman want to put on bunker gear and walk into a burning building?" The last "businessman" who joined the department was running for assemblyman. When he lost the campaign, he quit. Another local professional signed on to reduce his property taxes. The department created new requirements for active status to minimize these abuses. But the stigma of businessmen out for themselves remained. Peter had to prove himself worthy of the call.

Training was done by active and retired New York City firefighters. Peter went through many night classes, crawling through smoke-filled mazes, climbing seven-story ladders and studying hazardous materials. He wanted to be ready to help if we were attacked again. As a probationary firefighter (first-year probie), he found himself on an emergency call sitting next to a young firefighter. "I know you," the young man said. "I helped build your pool." The separation of economic classes in firefighting is vast. White-collar businesspeople and professionals do not ordinarily become volunteer firefighters. They answer the call for service in other important ways—giving to charities, forming foundations, sitting on boards. The dangerous job of protecting the community as a firefighter is usually reserved for the working class. As a CEO of a Wall Street search firm and a volunteer fireman in his community, Peter is a bridge between these two worlds. Through the rigorous first-year training, he developed a deep respect for the firefighters' work ethic. Professional off-duty firefighters, many of them decorated officers from the Fire Department of the

City of New York, donated their time and expertise to training the new recruits. They shared with them everything they knew. These seasoned heroes earned Peter's lasting admiration as he experienced their unwavering integrity.

Peter remained humble and devoted and the department gradually gained confidence in him. He became one of the most beloved and respected firefighters in this volunteer fire company setting a new standard for "probies." "You changed this department," said one retired New York City firefighter, a veteran of the infamous Father's Day Fire of June 2001. Peter's enthusiasm, passion and reverence for firefighting inspired them to see their own value through his eyes.

The job was even harder than it looked. It required enormous physical strength and fitness. A typical training session involved putting on 100 pounds of gear, a Scott Pack and oxygen mask stuffed with paper and crawling through a smoke-filled maze flat on their stomachs. Peter, who thought he was in top physical shape, struggled to keep up with his colleagues. As New York City was rebuilt by our uniformed brothers, Peter learned the meaning of trust in his evenings at Fire School. "No matter what, make sure you've got your brother's back." Trust was the foundation of the brotherhood.

We had experienced trust in business with long-time associates. These colleagues behaved like firefighters by keeping their word when it mattered most. We knew they could be counted on to "have your back." There was a large group of Wall Street businesspeople who earned loyalty and trust in this manner, yet it was an eye-opener how these individuals were often silenced by daily headlines about others in the business community who did not value the same code.

For many of us, business is an honorable profession. A close friend of Peter's and long-term client, Mike Mortara, the former head of fixed income at Goldman Sachs, was a businessman who had the heart of a firefighter. He instilled loyalty in everyone who knew him by honoring his word. His colleagues and subordinates knew he *always* "had their backs." His integrity proved that it was possible to achieve enormous financial success and be worthy of trust. For us, he represented the connection between the honor of firefighting and the dignity of business.

Money Doesn't Grow on Trees

When we speak around the country to non-business groups, we usually ask how many people present are "in business." A small percentage will raise their hands. People are loath to admit they are in business for fear of being vilified. Then we ask, "How many of you work for a living?" All hands shoot up. We point out that if you work for a business and get paid, you are part of the business, "for-profit" world. Even if you work for a nonprofit or the government, unless you are a volunteer you are still getting paid. Nonprofits and government depend on other people's money, in the form of donations and taxes for their operating costs. Without the profits of businesses and individuals neither entity would function.

Our purpose in detailing this is to highlight the need for each of us to profit. We are hypocritical if we have contempt for the foundation our livelihoods depend on. We become selectively judgmental when we decide how much is enough and for whom. We depend on profit for our survival. To profit is healthy and normal in our capitalistic world. When we work, we wish to earn money.

The American Dream

For far too long, "bad" business has been hijacking the reputation of everyone else, and consequently, business groups are embarrassed that the public mistrusts them. Businesses and managers want to learn how to change this perception and gain the public's confidence. Businesses are made up of people like you and me, and the outrageous antics of a small percentage of individuals create the negative image for all of us. Greenspan calls crooks in the business community "a distinct minority." At the 2005 Wharton Business School graduation, he stated, "We could not have achieved our current level of national productivity if ethical behavior had not been the norm."

In our view there isn't anything wrong with making lots of money. It is, after all, the American dream. Who should decide whether two hundred thousand, two million, or two hundred million dollars is the "right" amount for us except ourselves? Unlimited wealth hasn't created mistrust for people like Oprah Winfrey. We do not judge her based on her enormous wealth of more than a billion dollars. Instead we applaud her. She has created it by enhancing people's lives. This is our barometer of acceptable wealth. We trust Oprah; we don't feel betrayed by her. Bill Gates is another billionaire who many people feel has contributed greatly to our modern world. Yet our ten-year-old son's Bill Gates costume one Halloween created both awed and repulsed responses. One mother said, "Oh, gross, Bill Gates." We said we thought he was an admirable brand of billionaire. She replied, "Well, I guess his father does good things with his money." One particular author of business books calls Gates a "robber baron." When we noted that robber barons were known for their exploitation of workers and Gates is known for his exemplary treatment of workers, she responded with, "That's just my pet peeve." The resentment for wealth and business is so strong that it frequently becomes irrational. Yet business itself is responsible for much of these views—we have created mistrust by our own misdeeds.

Risky Business

"Can you trust Google with your secrets?" asked the cover of *Time* magazine in February 2006. That very week, the United States Congress and human rights groups were asking the same question of Google, Microsoft and Yahoo regarding their operations in China.

The federal investigation revolved around the ethics of Internet censorship by Communist China and the three tech giants. Why were these free-market capitalists cooperating with the Chinese government to shut down "controversial" blogs and compromise the confidentiality of e-mail users? Congressmen, including a holocaust survivor, compared these actions to the collaboration of IBM with Nazi Germany. Columnist Richard Cohen of the *Washington Post* wrote in response to the censorship, "Many an American fortune was based on the slave trade or exploitation of the Indians or some such atrocity."

The conclusion of the congressional committee was that neither Google nor the other companies could be trusted with anyone's secrets when profit-push came to profit-shove. The Google spokesman said he was not "ashamed," but not "proud" of his actions, but he had to follow Chinese laws. Microsoft said they were "deeply troubled" by the ethical conflict posed by their censorship. All three companies claimed that a manipulated and distorted Internet was better than none at all.

One could easily pass judgment on these companies as greedy and ruthless. However, it would contradict the image held of these companies as being models of Corporate Social Responsibility. The commitment of billionaire Bill Gates to give away 90% of his fortune to those in need speaks volumes of the humanitarian nature of Microsoft's leader. He and his wife, Melinda, devote extraordinary amounts of money, time and effort to help relieve worldwide human suffering.

Google's two founders are known for their ethical practices including adjusting standard IPO rules to represent
their personal value for integrity. Mavericks Sergey Brin
and Larry Page broke ranks with the mainstream corporate
world when they coined their now famous company motto,
"Don't Be Evil." These innovators understood that creating
trust among their users was the primary ingredient in long-
term success. Ruffling some corporate feathers along the way,
the two visionaries insisted on including the motto in their
public offering. They stated, "We believe strongly that in the
long term, we will be better served—as shareholders and in
all other ways—by a company that does good things for the
world even if we forgo some short-term gains." In doing so,
this multibillion-dollar profit engine changed the rules for
Wall Street itself.

The founders bravely carved out a new role model for
all other companies to follow. They seemed to be saying that
trust is everything. It's your bread and butter. Without it, you
jeopardize your own future.

Now both companies were operating in Communist
China, following the censorship "laws of the land" and
casting a shadow of mistrust over their well-honed public perception of honor. Why would morally accountable
people like these participate in the suppression of human
rights for profit? The common view among them is that
their presence in China will have a positive affect on the
culture. Better some access to information than none at all,
they claim. To date they have made moderate changes. Microsoft and Google thought long and hard about the issues
raised in the investigation and resolved to locate blog and e-
mail outside of China to insure future user privacy. Google
continues to follow Chinese mandates on their website,
but informs users that the site is censored. This disclaimer
has threatened Google's continuing operation in China by

angering the Chinese national press who claim the site is illegal. Yet those simple actions show both Microsoft and Google are attempting to do business in China without discarding their humanity.

In an ironic twist just one month after the congressional hearings on the tech companies and China, Google fought hard to protect online privacy rights on its home turf. In March 2006, a federal judge denied the United States Justice Department access to Internet search queries on Google claiming it would violate the trust customers have in the information giant. It remains to be seen whether Google can uphold the same standards of integrity in China without becoming "evil."

Yahoo on the other hand has claimed it cannot act similarly, as it merged with a Chinese company last year. Because of this, Yahoo stated it cannot reveal to U.S. representatives any of their dealings with the Chinese government. Reporters Without Borders blasted Yahoo for releasing confidential names of "cyber-dissidents" to Chinese officials. The journalists were imprisoned for eight and ten years respectively. Yahoo China now answers to the Chinese government rather than the U.S. government for its business practices. For all practical purposes, by refusing to honor U.S. values and laws, it seems Yahoo China has sold its American soul to the Chinese. While it is important to bring China into the global community, doing business there begs the question, at what cost will we profit? Will we compromise the value we place on human dignity and freedom for market share?

Socially responsible, worker-friendly companies like Timberland and Eileen Fisher produce some of their goods in China. Unlike the tech companies, these manufacturers insist on western-style fair labor standards for their Chinese workforce. Both companies (along with others operating in China) hire supervisory firms to insure workplace regulations are met. The result is that American fair labor practices are influencing Communist Chinese culture.

If we dangle the money carrot in front of our global economic partners and influence them to respect human rights, we have achieved something great. We have used money and commerce as a powerful force for social change. Yet if our zeal for profit forces us to change our basic value system and become like the tyrants we work for, then our hunger for money has distorted the very thing that made us great—free enterprise.

What are our fundamental spiritual values? Do we cherish human life and dignity? If so, we cannot cross that line to profit. We hold our basic value for human well-being as sacred when making difficult decisions. By doing so, we preserve the trust our customers and clients have for us.

Liar Liar

There's no need for us to point the finger at other industries, when we can examine our very own. Wall Street headhunting is often known for its lack of ethics. It's right up there with used-car salesmen, backstabbing realtors, dishonest stockbrokers and corrupt pension-fund managers. What often causes the industry to be disdained are some of the people in it and the lack of integrity they are known for.

Early in his career as a rookie for a large midtown search firm, one successful recruiter, a friend of ours, experienced it all. The company president told him in his first week of employment that whenever he looked at a potential client or candidate he saw a dollar sign across their face. Set up like a trading floor in a large bullpen of hungry recruiters, the competition was fierce. Quotas and production numbers were posted on the wall and commissions were paid only when the deal was done. Our friend sat next to an affable young man who lied from morning to night to candidates and clients alike. When asked why he made promises he couldn't keep, his colleague said, "I tell them what they want to hear." "But you're not telling them the truth," our friend insisted. "So? They don't know that." Both recruiters quickly became the largest producers at the company.

The recruiters later went on to create their own successful search firms, but each did this very differently. Our friend's view was to create trust with his clients. In contrast, he became known for telling them the truth even if it meant the deal would fall through. He prospered by serving his clients' needs. Through the years, he created a network of thousands of industry colleagues who knew he could be counted on. His belief was that if you honor your clients, they will honor you in return. One could, as many do, make plenty of money without this attitude. Yet Wall Street inevitably becomes a small world and reputation is everything. Loyalty can pay off handsomely. He has developed exclusive relationships with the heads of top financial institutions—firms that will only do business with individuals they trust.

On Your Honor

A veteran portfolio manager with an Ivy League education had carefully nurtured his career during the years he worked for an esteemed money-management firm. A well-known recruiting firm contacted him with an offer he couldn't refuse—to join a hedge fund as a credit trader headed by the former managing director of a major investment bank. The recruiting firm assured him the hedge-fund CEO was well respected as an industry giant. They further detailed how he had interviewed twenty-five candidates for the position and had not hired anyone due to his high standards. After the trader's initial interview the CEO offered him a job on the spot and asked him to start immediately. Unbeknownst to the trader, his new employer had a reputation for underhanded machinations. Within a couple of months, the CEO's trading funds were pulled. He claimed he would retool and asked the trader to wait for him, but the trader decided to interview instead. When a potential employer called the defunct CEO for a reference, he claimed the trader still worked for him. The hire was ruined because the trader looked untruthful.

When the trader contacted the recruiting firm to discuss how he should proceed, they insisted he wait for the CEO to start a new fund. The trader became convinced their only goal was to collect their unpaid commission—and they would sabotage his carefully orchestrated career to do it. Unfortunately for the recruiting firm, the trader relayed the scenario to his college roommate, a managing director at one of their main client firms. The headhunters were caught in the act and their dishonesty immediately cost them a high-paying client. Proof again that in business, reputation is gold.

A Sucker is Born Every Minute

In this world of instant information, there is far more opportunity to practice hit-and-run economics. The thinking in short-term business methodology is that there is a sucker born every minute, and therefore there will never be want of a customer. This manifested on Wall Street when analysts concerned with their own profits urged investors to buy sinking stocks. Consequently, all brokers, analysts, and market advisors are routinely assumed to be corrupt. Universal cynicism grows with each new headline.

Though business is often considered a foe, it is also considered a support system. We count on our corporations to employ as many individuals as possible. We are devastated when they close factories or lay off workers. When Bernie Ebbers was sentenced to twenty-five years in prison, a local financial analyst said, "It's a tragedy for all of us in Mississippi." Another resident said, "A lot of people relied on him for jobs and weren't expecting the company to go under." Many of our retirements are dependent on the good graces of public companies. We want to trust business. We want reasons to restore our faith in our business leaders. Yet all around us we are not being protected. We fear bad news daily. The pension you are sure of, the security you believe will be there when you need it, may not be. The job you depend on and have given years of your life to may be shipped off tomorrow.

Practice What You Preach

In 1943, long before it was fashionable, General Robert Wood Johnson wrote "Our Credo" for his company Johnson & Johnson. His maverick views broke with the profit-at-any-cost culture of the era, as Johnson called for "a new industrial philosophy." In order of importance, his credo ranks corporate responsibility first to customers, then to employees, communities, and finally to stockholders. The basic thinking of old man Johnson was that if you take care of customers through the quality of your products, profits will follow. The success of a company with annual sales exceeding $50 billion has proven the general right.

Companies often have values-based mission statements, and all too often they are only lip service to the outside world. Business writer John Kador claims in *Great Engagements* that Johnson & Johnson is committed to long-term growth by "valuing three varieties of capital—intellectual, social and human." In an early-1980s business conference with management guru Peter Drucker, a Johnson & Johnson executive in the audience asserted, "The purpose of business is to create customers and serve them ethically." Johnson & Johnson was tested on this very theme during the Tylenol-tampering crisis of 1982. Over a four-day period in the greater Chicago area, seven people died of cyanide poisoning inserted into Extra Strength Tylenol capsules. Putting "customer safety first," Johnson & Johnson immediately recalled and destroyed all varieties of Tylenol, their most profitable product. A new "tamperproof" version was shipped out within six months as a remarkable example of responsible corporate behavior. The CEO kept the public informed of their efforts and offered complete disclosure of the facts in the case. The company view was to sacrifice short-term profits for long-term loyalty. Their frankness and accountability helped them regain their most cherished financial asset—the trust of their customers.

In Business We Trust

Business is not our enemy; it is actually our friend. We depend on it for food, shelter, clothing, entertainment and comfort. It provides us with our livelihood and in turn, our standard of living. Can we trust it to serve us with honor and integrity? Perhaps most people would answer no. Those of us in business are greatly responsible for this as we have created it by our short-sighted avarice. The time has come for us to recognize the damage done.

It seems a step back in time is needed—to the days when a handshake was meaningful, when integrity was expected, and to combine that with a modern awareness for the ethical treatment of others. We could blend some old-fashioned honor with some new-fashioned compassion and create an empowering vision for the future. "I have a dream" that we will live to see the day where businesses are judged not only by the size of their profits but by the mark of their integrity.

◆

Lesson 7

The foundation of business is trust

*"Always act with integrity—
never follow the crowd."*

WARREN BUFFETT
BILLIONAIRE, MARKET MOVER

The foundation of business is trust

WHERE is the dignity in business? If we feel we are being exploited, lied to or cheated, there is none. This expands to any profession—law, medicine, manufacturing, advertising, sales or any others. Law, for example, used to be viewed as an honorable calling, very different from the view we have now. Scholarly dignity and integrity marked the old-fashioned practice of law. Our modern perspective is that of a shyster ready to fleece us. We constantly hear jokes about "lawyer" interchangeable with "liar." While there are many who function this way, there are still those who defend our rights, win just compensation, right society's wrongs and honestly advise us. Similarly, there is often an unrecognized dignity in doing business and making money. If we are selling a quality product or service, we are benefiting others as well as ourselves. Hard work and creative ingenuity equal good business—not deception.

The foundation for business is trust. One creates trust by establishing positive relationships with customers, suppliers, employees and clients; relationships are the essence of our business efforts and money is the by-product. We often hear, "It's not what you know, but who you know." Yet what is equally important is *how* you are known. Expanding and maintaining a business requires a proven track record of reliability. Your long-term success depends on your reputation, which is more important than top-notch advertising. Do you stand by your word or guarantee? We talk about our product quality and dependability. We claim, "You can depend on us." Yet do we practice what we preach? We are dependent on the continued support of our customers, clients, workers, shareholders, suppliers and communities for our very existence. Give them the best service or product you have and your future prosperity is assured with repeat business and referrals.

All products and services are ultimately serving a human need. Have we been honorable in the portrayal of our goods? Do we serve our clients and customers in the same way we would serve ourselves, our families and friends? Or are we nonchalant about deceptions in our business practices? Simply put, *can we be trusted?* The answer's impact on our bottom line is enormous. The most important factors in our long-term business goals are faith and trust. In order for business to be viewed as a trusted partner, we must restore faith in the institution. This begins at the very top with our business leaders.

Key Points in Lesson Seven

> Hard work and creative ingenuity equal good business—not deception.

> We create trust by establishing positive relationships with customers, suppliers, our workforce and clients.

> Money is the by-product of our business efforts, but relationships are the essence.

> Repeat business and referrals are what we strive for.

How Does Lesson Seven Manifest in Your Business Success?

Example #1

CEO, Search Firm

Not so long ago, a happy headhunter with two decades of relationships and experience behind him reached the pinnacle of his career. A large conglomerate made him an offer he couldn't refuse—to merge his small firm with their large one and he could stay at its helm. The buy-out firm was going public. In the first months of the IPO, his shares skyrocketed to $12 million. All those years of toil and long hours finally came to fruition; now he could sit back and coast a bit.

The union had opened many new doors for him professionally. Companies that would never retain his services were calling him due to his new status. Only he had one small challenge he didn't have before: as CEO of his own company he never had to answer to anyone other than himself, but now he had shareholders and a board of directors to report to. He must keep profits up or his shares would sink. He decided to take matters in his own hands when he heard of an upper-management position at a large commercial bank. He knew he could fill that spot quickly and reap hundreds of thousands of dollars in fees. He knew just the right candidate for the position, however, the candidate worked for a valued client of his new firm. This meant ethically as well as contractually he had to keep hands off. Yet this never stopped him before.

He plotted his strategy. "I will tell the candidate to keep it confidential. No one will ever know it was me," he thought. When the placement was made, everyone in the industry lauded it. Wow! What a coup! Who was behind it? News spread fast and tongues wagged. It was not long before the client firm discovered that one of their very own executives was responsible for losing this key player. The buy-out firm fired him immediately for breach of contract and he was left to salvage what remained of his tainted career.

EXAMPLE #2

INVESTMENT BANK BOND TRADER

A young man left his blue-collar background behind when his parents sacrificed to put him through college. Armed with the first business degree in his family, a college friend suggested he work on Wall Street. Watching his parents struggle financially as a child, he had vowed to help them as soon as he could. He was offered a trading job at an investment banking firm. Very quickly in his new position, he was able to reimburse the retirement money his folks had used for his college education. Before he knew it, he was making well over a million dollars. Yet he did not leave his humility behind. His father, who he respected more than anyone, had never earned more than $50,000 a year as a construction worker. In his son's eyes no one could hold a candle to him. He learned from his parents to be generous and honorable, and to never let money make you forget who you are or those you love.

As time went by, he earned a valued reputation as a trader in a notoriously competitive and cutthroat market. What was the secret to his success? Early in his career, one trade had left a client with a bond that nosedived immediately after he recommended it. The client was furious and believed the young trader had deliberately deceived him. The trader assured him he had not. To prove his point, he instructed the client to "tear the ticket up" and that he would not process it. Risking his own job, the young trader put honor before profit. The bond-buyer responded with, "You gained a client for life." He continued to earn the trust of clients and colleagues alike and has since reached the top in his field.

Applying Lesson Seven to Your Life

Trust is a delicate concept, easily damaged by imagined deceit, and so precarious and illusory we can shatter it in a moment. Though intangible, trust is carried firmly in our hearts and minds. When we trust something or someone, we *believe* in them. If people trust business to be honorable and responsible to their product or service, faith will be a natural by-product. For the sake of our future in this global age, we must shift the current perception that the majority of business is corrupt. Unethical business will always be there, but let it be the exception, not the norm. When business takes pride in its contribution to society, consumers will restore their faith in business-kind.

Tools for Including Trust in Your Business Life

› Make sure your word is your bond by honoring all agreements with clients, customers and colleagues.

› Stand by your product or service and represent it honestly.

› Nurture and cherish your best business asset—your reputation.

CREATING A VISION FOR TRUST IN BUSINESS

Be someone others can depend on. Create a history of reliability with clients and colleagues by being true to your word. Honor is upholding your promises and commitments. If you inadvertently wrong someone, promptly admit it and answer for it. Think in terms of longevity in business and not only short-term gains. Understand that the reputation of having integrity among customers, colleagues and clients is priceless.

◆

Chapter 8

All for One and One for All

"The leaders who work most effectively… never say 'I.' They don't think 'I.' They think 'we'; they think 'team.' They understand their job to be to make the team function. They accept responsibility and don't sidestep it, but 'we' gets the credit."

PETER DRUCKER
MANAGEMENT PROFESSOR

All for One and One for All

SEPTEMBER 11, 2001 claimed the lives of 343 firefighters. There might have been 344 if an extraordinary rescue had not occurred. His name is Alfredo Fuentes—a decorated veteran New York City fire captain who served with the famed Rescue 2 and Marine Divisions. As all hell broke loose on that September morning, Captain Fuentes stood near the North Tower trying to extricate close friend Chief Peter Ganci, fellow firefighters and civilians from beyond a glass wall in the remains of the Marriot Hotel. In front of his eyes, the building came down on his old friend, the firefighters and those he was struggling to save. And then it came down on him. As he lay buried under mountains of poisonous rubble, he thought of those he loved and those he had just lost.

In life's incomprehensible pattern, the captain had taken a "super radio" with him that morning. Since the 1993 attack of the World Trade Center, the New York Fire Department had discovered their radio dispatch system was tragically dysfunctional. It had failed to communicate in the extreme conditions of those high-rise buildings. In the eight years since, it had not been replaced with an adequate system. This cost many firefighters their lives on September 11. Captain Fuentes advised his men to carry a portable citywide radio in emergencies. His presence of mind saved his own life.

Fighting to stay conscious as he bled profusely from severe head wounds, a fractured skull, collapsed lung, shattered vertebrae, chemical burns and broken ribs, Captain Fuentes issued a call for help across the radio waves. He was convinced he would die there in the dust of hatred. The fire department radios lit up across the eerie silence: "Mobile command—requesting urgent help." The call of a "trapped fireman" galvanized firefighters from every direction. Dozens who had responded from home that morning began the grueling task of searching for the captain and other survivors. They were in rescue mode, virtually disregarding their own safety.

They call themselves "brothers" even though they have never met. Firefighters feel a bond through what they do that goes way beyond ordinary loyalty. They are unified in their rescue efforts—a cohesive unit built to save lives for the sole reason that this is what a firefighter does. They hold a deep allegiance to colleagues who similarly sacrifice their own needs by serving something greater than themselves.

On September 11, the brotherhood ran to the aid of downed Fire Captain Fuentes. They immediately formed a remarkable team, each one trained to know his part. The brothers crawled through the rubble at Ground Zero until the sleeve of a firefighter's coat was glimpsed beneath an enormous pile of debris. Perhaps they didn't know one another's names, but they knew something even more personal about each other: *that no firefighter would leave without the captain.* Each fireman instinctively took a task in the efforts to free him. It took several men to load the large injured man onto the stretcher. Many others carried him over several stories of rubble to the rescue boats on the shoreline. Inch by inch they gently dragged him along, careful not to re-injure him amid the fires and destruction around them. There were times they thought they could not muster another ounce of strength. "I'm going to drop him!" one firefighter yelled. "No, we're going to do it. We're taking this guy," another rescuer said. This quickly assembled team of firefighters rallied and carried on. They saved Captain Fuentes' life that day.

THE ROCK

Teamwork is the heart of the New York City Fire Department. Each expertly trained member of the brotherhood knows what to do in an emergency. They train, train again and then train some more. There is little room for mistakes in the real world. Their education is ongoing and rigorous. Fire School in New York City is called "The Rock" and is the equivalent of a firefighter's Ivy League. When they graduate, firefighters are able to respond to any real-life situation. One firefighter drives the truck, another ladders the building, another charges the line, another carries the tools until each member is doing his or her part to resolve the problem. Each one does his best and relies on the other members to do theirs.

A firefighter works with a buddy that "has his back" and watches over him. The New York City firefighter's motto is: "In unity there is strength." All members understand that the quality of the whole department depends upon every one of them. In order to *be* the best, they must *do* their best—as a team. The result is that the New York City Fire Department is among the most talented and extraordinary fire departments in the world. The essence of teamwork is what makes all fire departments effective. It is not about grandstanding, it's about unity.

Captain Fuentes lived to tell his story in a poignant memoir. He was forced to retire from his beloved FDNY due to severe injuries, but continues to be part of the team through his nonprofit organization, The Patriot Group, dedicated to helping firefighters throughout the U.S. stay safe. Another FDNY fire captain and 9/11 survivor, Dan Sheridan, formed Mutual Aid after the tragedy, a group dedicated to teaching fire departments in less affluent countries how to improve their safety and skills. Like firefighters everywhere, they are part of a greater brotherhood that holds humanity at its core.

Simply the Best

Some "spiritually minded" persons believe that competition is second only to greed and not conducive to harmonious workmanship. This theory is challenged in the face of the unified New York City Fire Department. They are arguably the best because they work hard at it. They are not the only great fire department, but their standard of excellence raises the bar for others.

There is a healthy side to competition that is necessary to success. In business, it is the thing that gets you out of bed in the morning. It drives you to improve your product and increase your bottom line. Department store magnate J.C. Penney says, "Competition is no enemy, it is an ally, and when translated into service, it is a constant spur to betterment through more service and thus benefits all." If you don't desire to accomplish great things, don't wish to excel at what you do, don't strive to be the best you can—you won't be. Desire to do your best is essential to personal achievement, and competition teaches you what you are capable of. For example, in sports, if you compete with someone better than you, your game improves. Runners always achieve their best time in races, because competing with others pushes them to do better.

Business mogul J.P. Morgan was hounded by President Teddy Roosevelt in the early twentieth century for his violations of antitrust law. The Sherman Antitrust act was enacted to break up economic monopolies that interfered with free-market enterprise. In response, Morgan uttered the famous line, "What's so great about competition?" Our free-market system depends upon competition. In its most productive form, competition encourages hard work and creative ideas. It does not have to be cutthroat. You do not have to destroy other rivals in your quest to succeed. Like a New York City firefighter, focus your attention on your own actions. The rest will follow.

STAR POWER

Everyone wants to be on a winning team. On Wall Street this is no different. A top Wall Street firm who understands that "in unity there is strength," functions very similarly to a well-oiled fire department. Every member of the team works for the good of the whole organization. We have worked for many years recruiting talent for top investment banks and money-management firms on the Street. We are privy to specific information about what each firm looks for in terms of education, work experience, personality, cultural fit, work ethic and character. We learned that there are basically two types of firms on Wall Street: team players and solo players.

Solo-player firms are often full of "stars" who work for their own benefit. These firms actively employ standout industry members who make huge amounts of money for the firm and perhaps have great impact on their sector but do not like to share the glory. These are very talented people who can be savage competitors to colleagues in their own firms as well as outsiders. There is a brutal quality of competition at these firms. Everyone you work with is suspect and would easily steal your ideas, profits, and even your clients if they could get away with it. The managers of these firms have little loyalty to their staff as they are former stars themselves who clawed their way up.

This is the common image of the financial community, as popularized by the 1980s Oliver Stone movie, *Wall Street*, along with the famous scandals of that era. These events were followed by a decade of books, television shows and movies incorporating the same themes. Everyone on Wall Street was thought to be a crook. Ruthless greed was heralded as the secret to success in the industry. The message for young Wall Streeters was that you must be willing to do anything in order to succeed—lie, cheat, steal, or whatever it takes to climb to the top of the money heap. How much money you made was the only barometer of success. How you made it was a non-issue.

For several years we recruited "star" talent for a solo-player firm. We staffed much of their mortgage-backed securities desk, and they were considered one of the top players in the field. Everyone we placed there had a certain "arrogance" to them. They were stars and wanted to be recognized for it. They would ask us, "How much are they going to pay me?" This is an important question, but it usually accompanies other questions about the culture of the firm and the character of the management. No one asked those questions at this firm because no one cared. Talent and a go-for-the-jugular drive were the only required qualifications. The "right stuff" meant you would trample anyone and anything that came between you and your profits. They had many stars but no team loyalty.

Were they successful? Hugely profitable. After all, they had a lot of "stars" who made a lot of money for the firm. We stopped working with them when one of the managers reneged on an agreement. He'd had a bad quarter and didn't make his quota on the desk. He had to get the money from somewhere, so he betrayed our trust (and that of many other contractors) after eight years of service. There was no loyalty for colleagues, clients or consultants; it was not part of the culture. From that point on, we made the decision to work only with firms who had clear integrity and loyalty. We wanted to be part of a team.

Team Spirit

Lest you think we were naive in our team spirit, we had something to compare this with. The contrast between the aforementioned "star" firm and our primary client was startling. There was never a conflict of interest for us between the two firms. Anyone that the star firm would hire, our main client would never hire. Anyone our main client wanted to hire would never work at the star firm. There was a clear separation of philosophy.

Our main client was a cohesive team of top industry talent. Investment bankers, managers, traders, salespeople, analysts—each member of the firm was a star in his or her own right, but always worked as a team player. The firm was renowned for its honor. Their word was their bond. Displays of ego were discouraged and rare. Instead, steady excellence was the norm. The result was that they were considered the best firm in almost every sector.

This firm showed us how to succeed in business by simply being good at what you do. From management down they were fair—to us, their employees and clients. They considered us part of the team and inspired our loyalty. We could count on them to honor their word. They had a cherished reputation to uphold. Their team attitude made it easy to recruit for them. Colleagues looked out for each other and "had their backs." The lowest-level workers were made to feel as important to the success of the firm as those at the top. People were clamoring to work there and be part of a winning team that valued its employees.

Competitors were envious. "How do they do it?" they wondered. The simple answer was, through old-fashioned values like integrity. Billionaire Warren Buffet once said, "It takes twenty years to build a reputation and five minutes to ruin it. If you think about that, you'll do things differently." This view mirrored the philosophy of our main client. Management motivated people by communicating in a direct way, outlining a common vision and valuing everyone for their contribution.

Questions were asked about the character of potential hires. Candidates needed not only money-making talent and economic know-how; they needed a solid reputation too. Managers hired those who could make the stringent cut, but who also understood that honor was as important as skill—not much different than their counterparts on the New York City Fire Department.

A Winning Team

Office "politics" are a great source of stress for many businesspeople. The lesser side of individuals surfaces when they believe another threatens their security. In turn, people might devise many schemes to unseat others at their firms. It is every man or woman for themselves. These issues commonly result from firms with indifferent top management, who might even encourage this conduct. However, this infighting frequently results in large employee turnover and diminished productivity. It is not cost-effective.

One investment bank's IT department was headed by an employee who had "difficulty" managing people. The bank believed he had important technical skills and was not easily replaced. Yet one-fourth of his staff quit in the course of a short-term project due to his angry outbursts and inability to value employees. Talented workers left the firm to work for competitors. Innovation was thwarted as they started from scratch with each new employee. His management inadequacy cost the firm money, time and talent, three things critical to their success.

CREATING A SHARED VISION

The responsibility rests in upper management's ability to communicate the company vision. What does the firm want to accomplish? How does it see itself in the marketplace? Where are the areas for improvement? How does it encourage innovation and growth? A "spiritually enlightened" business has to create an environment that empowers its workers. Are they part of a team, or solo players working for their own gain?

A few years ago, the German electronics manufacturing company, Elcoteq Communications Technology, saved one of its factories from bankruptcy under the inspired leadership of manager Ruediger Fox. Facing massive layoffs due to decreased sales, Fox focused his efforts on creating a team spirit between management and factory workers. He began by making employees aware of their productivity and value to the firm's bottom line. He posted quarterly sales reports alongside projected overhead costs for all workers to see. This enabled them to understand how their personal efforts directly affected their job security. Secondly, he tackled the antagonistic relationships between management and employees. Fox used anonymous surveys to get employee feedback. Workers were given free reign to offer criticisms and suggestions about management and methodology. Each comment was investigated and resolved. Any manager or worker that wasn't in sync with the team effort was let go. He held factory-wide meetings and explained the company vision for growth and innovation to the entire firm. The management and worker collaboration increased productivity by 20% the first year. Profits doubled over corporate projections. Not only did his visionary tactics prevent layoffs, the firm increased the workforce by 15% after the second year.

The Golden Rule

In the last twenty years, new powerhouse corporations have emerged as leaders in the business community. As these public companies expand rapidly, they are changing the rules for business. Starbucks, whose enormous growth has captivated the market, refers to employees as "partners." Workers are paid above industry standard and given top-quality health and dental insurance. Through their stock incentive plans and stock option grants program, *partners* can become owners.

Silicon Valley companies like Microsoft and Google began their phenomenal success with built-in team ethics. The theory that two heads are better than one seems to resonate with Google founders Brin and Page. According to Google's Ten Golden Rules, team building, decision by consensus and hiring by committee are basic practices. Microsoft and many profitable tech firms function this way. They hire the best, and work people hard. In return these companies give employees a stake in the profits and every imaginable employee perk, from health clubs to dry-cleaning to daycare. Applicants clamor to work at these companies.

Business management used to set all the rules for employees. Nowadays successful corporations partner with their workforce to create a better environment. Maverick leaders like Howard Schultz of Starbucks and John Mackey of Whole Foods seem to understand the basic economic rationale that a satisfied workforce equals a more productive one. At Whole Foods, Mackey calls his workforce "team members." He says, "If you don't have happy team members, you won't have happy customers. If you don't have happy customers, you don't have happy shareholders."

A Union of the Mind

Despite the seemingly worker-friendly environments Schultz and Mackey try to create, attempts to unionize their shops have overshadowed some of their efforts. Historically unions emerged due to the harrowing working conditions of the late-nineteenth and early-twentieth centuries. Cultural attitudes towards workers started to change in response to the vicious greed of Gilded Age industrialists. After the abolition of slavery, the need for those on the bottom economic rung of society to be protected from cruel employers was slowly recognized. This shift didn't happen bloodlessly, nor did it happen overnight. Upton Sinclair's shocking novel *The Jungle* exposed abominable working conditions in the meat-packing industry. The devastating Triangle Shirtwaist Fire in New York City, and other workplace tragedies, helped shape public views. Organizations that represented worker rights evolved from the sadistic practices of powerful industrialists. In the late 1800s workers who tried to unionize were often killed for their efforts. Government policies clearly favored the employers and many times declared labor organizing to be illegal. Fifty years of worker strife and violent revolts finally culminated in the establishment of worker unions that protected the workforce from employer exploitation.

The "touchy-feely" work environment of Starbucks seems to defy this scenario of a corrupt business ripe for unionizing. The company states firmly "that our progressive, positive work environment, coupled with our outstanding compensation and benefits, make unions unnecessary at Starbucks." Yet in one Manhattan store disgruntled workers brought an action against the company with the National

Labor Relations Board. After much talk and feuding, Starbucks agreed to the terms of the unhappy workers. This included rehiring two labor organizers and settling a back-pay suit of less than $2,000. "Our workforce is the soul of the business," Schultz said in response to the unionizing efforts. So far, the majority of Starbucks workers seems content with their unusually progressive corporate benefits and have not supported a union.

Worker unions often have mixed reviews from members. For example, New York firefighters complained that their union collected dues for several years in the prosperous 1990s yet failed to negotiate a new contract. However, employees often would not have basic needs met, such as pensions and health benefits, if unions didn't fight for these. But just because a union claims to represent workers doesn't mean that they do not have other agendas in mind. A worker in one well-known restaurant chain claimed she voted to unionize to end abusive work conditions only to find herself under the thumb of a gangster-controlled union.

Labor organizers have been guilty of the same exploitation and greed that they claim to rescue workers from. Criminal behavior of top management, such as excessive pay, perks, bribes and kickbacks for union bosses, lack of financial accountability and transparency, are just some issues plaguing unions that are remarkably similar to their capitalist corporate counterparts. After all, unions with thousands of members are "big business" too and prone to the same acts of corruption. Some pro-union activists claim unions are not prone to financial exploitation as they are "nonprofit." Yet until recently, the New York Stock Exchange was also a non-profit organization. This fact hardly prevented CEO Grasso from receiving $140 million in compensation.

Employers have told us that union demands have crushed their business and forced them to outsource. In theory and practice, many unions are necessary as they provide a check and balance on corporate greed. As always there seems to be abuses on both sides as unions, like corporations, are run by imperfect humans.

PARTNERS IN PROFIT

Generally in a team atmosphere, workers are not in need of unions. John Mackey, CEO and founder of the rapidly expanding Whole Foods Markets was shocked by one store's successful unionization: "Unions are not a good thing. They are resistant to change and they create an adversarial relationship to management. We think unions would be very harmful to our business." Management naturally prefers to deal directly with their workforce and doesn't enjoy third-party interference. Mackey's worker-friendly environment seemed to defy the need for a union until 2002, when a Madison, Wisconsin store voted 65-54 to unionize. Mackey wrote in an open letter to employees that he chose to "expand into love" rather than "contract into fear." He called the union vote a "wake-up call" to make his company "a better place to work." Since then, he allows team members in all his stores to vote for which benefits they prefer.

The question is not whether unions are right or wrong. Surely some unions offer important and necessary protection while others sadly exploit workers themselves. The issue for "spiritually minded" employers is how to balance the need for profits with the human needs of workers. As the cases of Whole Foods and Starbucks reveal, listening to employees is the first step. If basic human dignity is valued and assured, unions will commonly not appear; if they do, they can function in unison with an employer if both sides approach it that way.

A union does not have to be a business adversary. In today's marketplace, with outsourcing as a legal alternative to American labor, unions would be wise to represent their membership with a more conciliatory attitude to management. Similarly, companies can function in a mutually beneficial way with unionized workers. When a company expands to include thousands of workers in different locations, a manager or CEO has to do "double duty" to insure that worker-friendly policies are enforced. Corporations should not wait for the "wake-up call" to value their workers in word and deed. As CEO Howard Schultz said, employees are the "heart and soul of the company."

SPIRIT AT WORK

What would spirit at work look like in a Fortune 500 company with over 30,000 workers? Looking around the U.S. marketplace it might resemble the booming company of Southwest Airlines. The thirty-four-year-old, low-cost airline embodies the essence of teamwork and partnership in the pursuit of profit. Employees hold 10% of the company's stock and act like owners in the daily course of their jobs. Saving money, going the extra mile to keep things running smoothly and customers happy are the focus of every worker from top executives on down. The upper management created by founder and chairman Herb Kelleher and president Colleen Barrett puts employees (union and non-union) first in order of importance, customers second. Shareholders reap the benefits when the first two are cared for. Their theory seems to hold true as *Money* magazine named Southwest one of the 30 Best Stocks in 2002 with annualized returns exceeding 25%. And this was *after* September 11.

These attacks that used commercial airplanes as weapons devastated the airline industry. Several of the major airlines went bankrupt. The government had to step in to prevent an industry-wide economic collapse. Not surprisingly, airlines eliminated over 100,000 jobs and cut back on crews and flight schedules—with the exception of Southwest. As unbelievable as it might seem, the airline did not eliminate flights *or* people. Southwest Airlines did not lay off one person after 9/11. President Barrett said, "It was a given that we would not lay anyone off." A "given" not to cut costs with the workforce in a disaster marketplace like post-9/11? Defying all strategy to the contrary as taught in core management courses in MBA programs across the nation, former CEO Kelleher set the model for the company: "Nothing kills your company's culture like layoffs." People before profits? Is Kelleher brilliant or crazy? Many business writers and economists believe him to be one of America's best CEOs. *Fortune* magazine journalist Kenneth Labich called Kelleher "a people-wise manager who wins where others can't." In 2005, the airline ranked 318 on Fortune's 500 list and enjoyed their thirty-third year of profitability. Obviously, Kelleher's people-first policy pays off handsomely.

Just because they are worker-friendly does not mean they don't value hard work. Management expects a lot from its workforce and holds employees to their own standards. Dedication and collaboration are rewarded by profit-sharing and rare job security. Close to 80% of employees are unionized. Rather than taking adversarial positions, negotiations are mostly productive. In his book, *Faith and Fortune*, author Marc Gunther relates Southwest's upper management devotion to "servant leadership." Former AT&T executive Robert K. Greenleaf coined the phrase "servant leadership" in 1970, detailing how leaders are in service first, and then lead others from that perspective. Greenleaf claimed individuals mistrust organizations who strive to manipulate and coerce; in place of destructive persuasion, he advocated service as the spiritual essence of management.

Southwest's Kelleher and Barrett seem to innately understand their spiritual task as leaders in service. Basic principles that guide Southwest and its management include uncommon business values such as respect for others and following the Golden Rule. Says Barrett, "For us... the way you treat people is a way of life." Their mission statement reads, "Above all, Employees will be provided the same concern, respect, and caring attitude within the organization that they are expected to share externally with every Southwest Customer." The airline by all accounts practices what it preaches. An ethic of partnership and teamwork lays the foundation for the company's extraordinary success. Southwest found a way to serve two masters: higher purpose and profit.

Divine Prosperity

CEO and corporate reformer J-Robert Ouimet holds a particular team vision in his firm. The company generates over $110 million in gross annual revenues. "We call it a workplace so there is work done by human beings. For me each person has been created and loved by God. Therefore, the workplace is a precious place," he says. Human life is precious to Ouimet; therefore he believes that employees should be honored accordingly. His companies employ several hundred workers and implement innovative spiritual management methods. For example, new employees and managers break bread together along with their spouses or companions. The purpose of these meetings is to create a deeper human connection by seeing each other outside of the workplace. Spiritual capitalist Ouimet says that good employers must understand that "workers work to live not live to work." This viewpoint encouraged him to structure his factories to represent the interests of both employers and employees. His fair employee treatment stresses "just salaries and social benefits." Among the many employee perks is a "meditation" room offering silent sanctuary to all company personnel.

When we visited Montreal recently, Ouimet shared with us an important conversation he had with spiritual guide and mentor, Mother Teresa. In response to questions about the proper way to handle his great wealth, the saint told him to "manage it with God." First priority, Mother said, was to his wife, second to his four children, third to employees and their families and fourth to the larger world. Ouimet has honored that holy command in the two decades since by the "spiritual management" of his companies and traveling the globe to deliver his message of compassionate capitalism.

The Best is Yet to Come

Some 3,000 innocent people died on September 11, 2001—the result of many decades of events that finally ended in this great human tragedy. But more than 25,000 were rescued that day thanks to the phenomenal teamwork of the Fire and Police Departments of the City of New York and the dozens of other agencies who assisted. Every firefighter we knew who was not officially working that day went down to help at the disaster. Off-duty cops, firefighters, doctors and nurses were on the scene. Triage units were immediately set up around the site by area hospitals and hundreds of volunteer medical personnel. Even unrelated professionals like chiropractors, massage therapists, restaurant owners and psychiatrists lent their services. Everyone pooled their talents together that day and in the months to come. It was this combined effort that saved those 25,000 lives. All of America and the western world became Team 9/11. Money poured in from around the globe. Heartfelt letters, thoughts and sympathies were posted in editorials and web pages. We survived it together because we worked for a common purpose.

Wall Street too worked as a team in those months. Individually we looked out for each other, assisted families who lost loved ones, helped those who lost jobs and worked together to save our sanity. The Wall Street community and the fire department became permanently connected that day. Large and small investment banks bankrolled victims' funds and continue to this day to sponsor firefighter assistance programs.

We admire the New York City Fire Department because they are a great team *and* they have heart. They accomplished a remarkable feat through extraordinary circumstances by rescuing and rebuilding a city after huge personal losses and transcending the odds. They did it with dignity, honor and integrity making this the new standard of excellence for us all. To a firefighter *each and every* life is precious. Following in their footsteps these past four years, how could we ever be anything less again?

A Higher Purpose

Firefighters do not separate themselves from their humanity. They view their work as something sacred. In doing his or her job, a firefighter does not disconnect what they do from their greater purpose in the world: these are one and the same. Their unity to each other creates their connection to all of humankind.

In business, we often believe ourselves to be separate from humanity. This can result in us becoming "inhuman" to those we interact with. Hundreds of years ago, workers were called serfs and believed to be born for this lowly status. The huge exodus to America changed that dynamic for those who came here—suddenly you could overcome your poor roots and create a prosperous future.

Colonial America brought something else into the modern world. Slave ownership of other human beings for the sole purpose of free labor. These individuals were not the spoils of war; they were captured and imprisoned specifically for the purpose of profit. When the financial institution of slavery ended, industrialization began a new period of exploitation. Workers were treated by employers similarly to the master-and-slave model.

Gradually, an enlightenment began to take place. The next century brought with it worker rights that had never before existed. Unimaginable concepts emerged, like labor boards, unions, wage minimums, affirmative action, worker's compensation, and disability. A great corporate structure grew from this change in thinking. Loyalty to employers was rewarded with loyalty to workers. Pensions, vacation pay, health insurance and job security were added to the mix. With time our spiritual relationship to each other changed and improved.

Unfortunately, in the early twenty-first century, the current climate of indifference to workers represents a backward movement. The elimination of worker benefits and job security is reminiscent of less-evolved capitalism. However, powerhouse corporations like Starbucks, Whole Foods, Southwest, Google (U.S.), and Microsoft prove that the ancient spiritual ethic of the Golden Rule remains the modern model for success.

Teamwork and partnership are necessary qualities for businesses operating at the highest spiritual level. Business leader and publisher Steven Forbes says, "We are here on this earth and in this land for a higher purpose: to discover and develop to the fullest—our God-given potential." In caring for each other in our lives, our world and workplace, we have begun.

◆

Lesson 8

Teamwork is the heart of business

"A man is successful in proportion to the extent to which he encourages men to develop themselves. It really takes a big man to believe in other men, to entrust one's affairs to them, and having done so to discharge anxiety from the mind."

JAMES CASH PENNEY
BUSINESS MOGUL

Teamwork is the heart of business

HUMAN life is sacred. If we understand that life is sacred, then it logically follows that the workplace is sacred, as it is a manifestation of human existence. Honoring human dignity should be one of the main considerations when creating a work environment. Workplaces that do not cherish human beings dehumanize them. In a spiritually enlightened business, people are treated well. Therefore, employers and employees form a spiritual partnership. We are honor-bound to value each other and the trust our relationship entails.

Management has the great task to create a vision for the company. Simply crunching numbers and cracking a figurative whip will not motivate people. Leaders have the responsibility to share the bigger picture with employees. What is the higher purpose of the company? What are we doing here in the name of profit to serve the needs of human beings? These questions all form the basis for a practical vision. Focus on providing the best service to customers and clients, motivate your workers to do the same, and profits will follow.

We are human beings, not machines. People want to know their jobs are valuable. They desire to have pride in what they do. Let workers know where they fit into the bottom line.

Show them how their quality of work and productivity lead to company profits and in turn their own compensation. Managers usually know this about their jobs, but lower-level workers invariably do not. All of us need to feel valued as much in our work lives as we do in our private lives. We want to be recognized and rewarded for hard work, efforts and contribution. This is a simple human reality. Creating profits with purpose and passion is how we value the human spirit at work. Employers who expect loyalty from employees must offer the same in return. Inspire others to join the vision with fair compensation, benefits and a pleasant working environment. In turn, quality employees will give their best to the job asked of them.

KEY POINTS IN LESSON EIGHT

›   The workplace is a sacred place as it is a manifestation of human existence.

›   Management must create, communicate and inspire employees to a shared vision.

›   Employers and employees form a spiritual partnership.

HOW DOES LESSON EIGHT MANIFEST IN YOUR WORK LIFE?

EXAMPLE # 1

GLOBAL COMMERCIAL BANK

Managers at this commercial bank view employees similarly to the way cowhands view cattle. They crack the whip and keep everyone moving in a forward direction. The fact

that they have little innovation to show for their last de-
cade of business is no surprise. Quality control, customer
satisfaction and long-term employment are all non-issues as
the focus at this firm is short-term gains. Any job that can
be outsourced, is. The remaining workers are often told that
their jobs are not secure. They are expected to work longer
and longer hours for less money and benefits. Employees are
encouraged to betray the confidence of coworkers. Displays
of rage and intolerance among group leaders are the norm.
Each manager is criticized and pressured by their man-
ager, and in turn passes this down to the employees. The
company is run on a culture of fear. Employee turnover is
among the highest in the industry. Pensions are mostly a
non-issue as the majority of workers are laid off before they
are fully vested. Management, however, never neglects its
own future and pays itself handsome pensions and perks.

Even top management changes often, as the bank is known
for its love of mergers. Top executives pocket the "change
of control" fees with each buyout after only a few years
of service. It is not unusual for top execs to glean several
million dollars from company mergers that leave 5,000-
10,000 workers without jobs. Mergers are not done for
company security but to satisfy individual desire for profit.
In a little over a decade, the firm has experienced several
changeovers. Tens of thousands of workers have been dis-
placed, denied pensions, and left behind. There are no plans
to change this methodology as they still rank among the
world's richest banks.

EXAMPLE #2

LARGE SOFTWARE MANUFACTURER

*According to this highly successful software company, em-
ployees are directly related to the bottom line. On its website, the company calls its workforce "human capital." A
deliberate effort is made to attract the best people in the
industry by offering job perks such as child care, free on-
site health care, profit sharing and flexible work hours.
In their view, high employee turnover is expensive in re-
cruitment and retraining. Worker benefits are an economic
trade-off to maintain a productive workforce. The company
claims that the best investment it can make is in its people.*

*Employee turnover is less than 5% a year. Even in eco-
nomic downturns, employees are kept and new ones hired
to prepare for an eventual market upswing. The chairman of the company views downturns as temporary. He
cuts costs elsewhere, accepting fewer profits rather than
reducing a highly productive staff. The philosophy is one of
partnership with employees. Employees are rewarded for
good service with affordable and desirable retirement options. The view from the top down is that employees serve
the company with their best efforts. In turn, the company
repays employees with a stellar quality of life. The result
is the company's huge competitive advantage in a marketplace that often has high-volume worker turnover.*

APPLYING LESSON EIGHT TO OUR BUSINESS LIVES

Businesses, families and whole civilizations are created from
teams of people working for a common vision. Our collective
energy creates every institution. The difference between one
company or corporation and another boils down to the group

who functions in competition with one another or the team who functions in unity with each other. A winning team is one that has a clear, compelling, shared vision.

Tools for Including Teamwork in Your Workplace

› Create a "big picture" for all team members of where the company is headed.

› Show employees how their productivity fits into the bottom line.

› Value workers by showing concern for their personal needs.

Creating a Shared Team Vision

Communicate expectations to all employees. Detail how each of their efforts is crucial to the success of the whole venture. Know the strengths and weaknesses of team members and assign job duties accordingly. Inspire all workers with direct communication, enthusiasm and recognition. Create a spirit of camaraderie by letting workers know what their stake is in the future of the company. Encourage a high level of commitment by valuing the humanity of all employees.

Chapter 9

A Brave New World

"If we have no peace, it is because we have forgotten that we belong to each other."

MOTHER TERESA

SAINT

A Brave New World

WHEN the invisible walls that separate us daily came down on September 11 with the walls of the Towers themselves, we became one in our purpose: to help each other through this disaster. Through our mutual need to survive, we were left with only our essential selves and concern for each other. Trauma, it seemed, was a great equalizer. Strangers on the streets of the city opened their hearts with abandon to minimize the suffering of others. Our mayor became the voice of the people, sharing our grief and horror. His comforting strength gave us courage in those first months following the attack. New York City became a community that day. We were transformed.

On September 10, 2001, the word *community,* when applied to Wall Street, referred to a group of individuals in a common industry. For Wall Street, daily life was a relentless competition. Whoever got the most won. Common activities on the Street included calculated deceptions and fierce battles of wits, a world of economic gladiators. It was firm against firm. Even internally, employees were pitted against each other. Some of us created our own inner circle of colleagues, people we could count on in a pinch. Yet the nature of our world was not always open to trust. That wasn't the code. The code implied that you were only as good as your last trade. Ego and money were the motivating factors on the daily playing field. Vulnerability on Wall Street meant you left yourself open to attack from colleagues and competitors alike. However, on September 11, 2001, due to an attack by neither colleague nor competitor, we were vulnerable indeed. Suddenly ego had no place in our world. Money was second to survival and community was all that we had. Former competitors became allies and strangers became friends. Now they were colleagues in a community that depended on their cooperation and support for survival.

Another Wall Street

On September 12, the chairman of one of the world's largest investment banks stood staring at the ruins of his firm near the World Trade Center. He vowed that no matter what the cost might be, his firm would not go back there. He had no way of knowing whether insurance would pay for this destruction. Looking at the horror before him, he chose not to subject his firm to any further anguish by returning there. The chairman of a rival investment bank, a long-time adversary and competitor, heard of his plight and made an extraordinary gesture: without hesitation, he offered to give his office space on Park Avenue to the devastated investment bank, at a fraction of its cost. Months later, when it was confirmed that insurance would cover the losses completely, the chairman of the damaged firm offered to pay his supporter full market value for the Park Avenue office. With an unprecedented act of compassion from a direct competitor, the supporting chairman refused this offer. He stated that the firm had suffered so many losses through the tragedy that this was the least he could do to help.

Actions like this became commonplace in the financial community after the attack. Mirroring the rescue and recovery workers around them, Wall Street responded in kind. It seemed that this tragedy had the power to change even seasoned adversaries into friends. It was a sobering reminder of what was truly important: money, or life itself. Very few among us would ever be the same again. The secular indifference Wall Street was known for and the feeling of immortality that often came with wealth evaporated that fateful day.

The Brotherhood of Business

As Wall Street recreated itself in the shadow of their rescuers, the firefighters themselves depended on their existing community to pull them through the disaster. Anytime a firefighter acts in the line of duty, his comfort, safety and life are dependent on the cooperation of his colleagues. Firefighters are as human as the rest of us. However, when functioning in their official capacity, they put aside self-interest and work for the common good. If one person suffers, they all do. Putting their own needs first would jeopardize everyone involved including the larger community they serve. Every firefighter knows that if they do not care about the preservation of others, their own well-being is compromised.

Perhaps we don't realize it, but the indifference of business to the larger community compromises our own well-being. Business does not operate in a vacuum. It functions as a community within, and exists in a community without. Obligation to others is a basic part of doing business.

It's Only Natural

Although money and business are commonplace in our world, we view them as unnatural. Yet both emanated from our basic instinct to survive. In our early existence, humans traveled the world looking for food and shelter. When our ancestors realized they could create their own food and shelter, they stopped moving and developed societies where they were. Crops were grown and harvested, homes were built. Tribal members functioned together as their lives depended on it. In our first system of barter, people traded products like rice and grain that came directly from the land. Gradually humans developed a form of exchange based on precious metals like silver and gold. Trees yielded the paper we use today in place of gold and silver. The origin of money is nature itself.

Business is an organic human enterprise. It begins with an idea. We conceive of a product or service first and then we create it. We use the concrete result of our ideas to generate money for exchange. All human activity is derivative of nature as we are of nature ourselves. We seem to have forgotten in our common understanding that money and business are natural by-products of our human existence.

Life Cycling

In all of nature, there is a symbiotic relationship—what we call the cycle of life. Nature is made up of continuous actions and reactions. Everything that occurs in the natural world affects something else. When plant life uses carbon dioxide from the air, it releases oxygen for animals, including us, to breathe. The trees and all that is green sustain us. Why would we destroy the very things we depend on for our survival? This would be self-defeating.

However, global warming is just that—the human interference of the life cycle that sustains us. This warming is due to climate changes from an overabundance of carbon dioxide released into the atmosphere. Some scientists argue that this climate change is a natural phenomenon. Others claim it is the result of huge amounts of air pollution. To deny that humans have a part in global warming is to deny the very basis of nature itself. All actions have a reaction. Releasing large amounts of toxic fumes into the air would obviously affect it. Business has been slow to catch up with this natural logic. Only recently are giant energy companies beginning to research their affects on the environment.

A Shared World

In our communities we have rules regulating public places. When we picnic in a public park, we clean up after ourselves. If we left our garbage behind, the next visitors would feel intruded upon. We are obligated to leave the park as we found it, because we share it with others. It does not belong to us alone.

The same rules that apply to us individually apply to business. The world that business operates in is our shared world. When a company pollutes the air, the sea, the land that we live on, it affects everyone. A business might mistakenly believe that since its primary obligation is to shareholders, it can ignore its responsibility to the environment—forgetting that we all share in that legacy. Perhaps we may not reap the financial benefits, but we certainly reap the damage to our environment a company leaves behind. All of us are shareholders in our natural world.

The earth is a gift for us while we are here. We only borrow it for our lifetimes and leave it for others when we depart. We are visitors in this world, not owners. We did not create the earth, ourselves or anything in nature. Therefore, we have no right to destroy it. Whatever we take out of it, we must replace and leave it for the generations to come.

This simple spiritual logic is at the heart of the issue to care for our world. Our responsibility to the environment transcends politics, economics and religion. It is not a liberal-versus-conservative issue, nor a business-versus-general public issue. It is a basic spiritual issue of people who care about others versus those who don't.

And God Created the Earth

The devastation and utter human misery caused by Hurricane Katrina served as a wake-up call for those of us with a soul. If the science of global warming is correct, then we in business are partners in this crime against humanity. Too much evidence points to the conclusion that we are contributing to a serious climate change by our indifference to the balance of nature. As we drive down our highways, witnessing the fumes of black and grey pouring into the sky, we wonder where it all goes. Perhaps we thought it dissipated through the atmosphere. Perhaps we thought no further about it at all. Yet poisonous gases must go somewhere. We don't need to be scientists to understand this. It's basic common sense.

In early 2006, called to action by the suffering of Katrina victims, a group of evangelical ministers spoke out about our responsibility to preserve the balance of nature. Historically silent on an issue that had long been viewed as a flight of fancy by environmentalists, the Evangelical Climate Initiative suggests a growing general awareness of our contribution to the changing climate. The group states that we have "a sacred responsibility to steward the Earth and not a license to abuse the creation of which we are a part." Aren't we all environmentalists if our existence depends on the environment? The greening of America and American business should be a combined effort by everyone.

In the Judeo-Christian culture, there is a fundamental belief: "God created the Heaven and Earth and everything in it and gave us dominion over it." As a society we have somehow interpreted that as the right to abuse and deplete our world rather than cherish and protect it.

Hinduism, Buddhism and Native American religions see nature as part of the Divine itself. Islam teaches that we are "trustees" of the earth. Whatever your belief system, nature is sacred for all of us. We walk along a beach and the power of the ocean awes us. We stand among the mountains and are humbled by their majesty. We bring children into the world and are moved by the miracle that is life.

Our job is to cherish the sacredness in all things that exist—the stars above, the vastness of the sea, the baby in our arms, the mysteries left to uncover. We are guardians of an ancient and magical world. With that charge comes tremendous responsibility. Bill Gates, as head of one of the world's most profitable businesses, said, "There is a certain responsibility that accrued to me when I got to this unexpected position." And so it is for each of us—to life itself.

Its Not My Problem

Business has tremendous power over us. It is the engine that runs our material lives. It creates great personal freedom as we use our cell phones, computers and cars. It flies us in planes across the world, delivers products to our doorstep, brings food to our tables, puts roofs over our heads, designs our towns, motivates our politicians and shapes our thinking.

Although in business we have the power to create or destroy, we are often indifferent. We worry about ourselves. We make money, increase our market share, produce our products and leave the rest to others. As the five famed oil companies stated in the wake of Hurricane Katrina, they owed nothing more and nothing less to society than serving their shareholders. Altruism was not part of the financial plan. But in serving their shareholders they forgot that we are among them. We have an interest in the results of their efforts.

It's a big bad world out there. Our First Responders have a clear obligation to care for others. Business, however, believes it does not. What *does* business owe the larger community that does not support our bottom line? We wonder at Timberland's commitment to potable water or Bill and Melinda Gates' work to vaccinate children and ask, "What do any of those problems have to do with us?"

There is no requirement in our imperfect world to be concerned citizens. We can turn the other cheek. Mind our own business. Take care of ourselves and our families. Go on about our lives and not worry about the plight of the masses. We can leave the needs of others up to our government and our religious institutions. After all, we did not create these concerns nor can we fix them. It is not our problem... or is it?

The Sin of Apathy

When the nation witnessed the suffering of thousands in the wake of Hurricane Katrina in August of 2005, we despaired with them. The proud and fabulous city of New Orleans was a disaster waiting to happen. Ordinary people had no idea they were living in their own tombs. The hurricane hit with such ferocity that some say, as polluters, we were all partly to blame. The man-made levees crumbled beneath the force of the waves to the shock of the masses but not to those who built them. They knew—the engineers, politicians and businesses that built the levees *knew*. As we looked on, we could no longer turn the other cheek. This was barbaric; this was inhuman; this was inexcusable in our modern world. Avoidable human tragedies like this did not happen in a rich, powerful nation like ours, with all the innovation and modern technology at our fingertips... or did they?

The unfortunate answer was yes. Somehow with all the technological advancements available to us, none were implemented in New Orleans. Why? Very simply, to save money. It would cost too much money to build new levees. Too much money to have a disaster plan ready. Too much money to relocate local residents. Too much money to move the elderly and disabled to higher ground. Too much money to empty nursing homes and hospitals. Too much money to send doctors and nurses in to assist. Too much money to fly planes in to save the victims. Too much money to perform rescues for those stranded. Too much money to value human life *more*. As the number of lives lost grew, we understood. They were sacrificed for money.

The indifference of our leaders at all levels only made our frustration greater. Who could we count on? Not our public agencies. Nor our emergency systems. Our government had failed us. In our own apathy we turned away and left it to others to fill in the gaps. But now they crumbled along with the levees. Who was left to protect us if not the institutions we created to do so? Was it even realistic to expect them to do a job that belonged to all of us? Was it reasonable to expect privileged government appointees to safeguard the common man? Perhaps it *was* reasonable. Yet it was this expectation that cost many more lives. The devastating tragedy of Hurricane Katrina revealed that in truth we are all our brothers' and sisters' keepers. In our hearts and minds, we know we cannot turn the other cheek to their pain.

In the end it was our churches, our civic and community organizations, our public heroes like Oprah Winfrey, and the ordinary heroes of everyday people who came to the rescue. Wealthy observers donated millions in aid. Compassionate corporations and small businesses rushed in to fill the void left by our impotent leaders. The heroism of doctors and nurses who refused to leave their patients was measured against those who left their patients to die.

In the depths of our souls we knew we were all somehow responsible. We had not wanted to look, to know, to help. We were not bad people—we were good people. But we didn't create the problem and we couldn't fix it... could we? We don't have an obligation to help others... do we? It is not our problem... is it?

As we watched people drown in the diseased waters, thousands more pleaded for help. Old people, young people, beloved grandparents, terrified children, loyal pets—all helplessly anguishing right in front of us and none of us could reach through the television screens to assist them. We watched them tragically suffer and perish. Families split apart forever as all the powers in charge failed them. We found out that week and in the days that followed that it is up to all of us to care for each other. Because if not us... then whom?

In the future when the question comes up again about what the social obligation of business is to the greater community, we will remember Katrina and our deep desire to help the victims. We will also remember September 11 and how all of us became First Responders. These tragedies have taught us something very important about ourselves—that we *do* care. We do feel a social and spiritual responsibility to others and what exists beyond ourselves. We know now that it is the same for us individually as it is for our government *and* our businesses—to care for those less fortunate, to be of service in our communities, to help lift the burden of living for others as we go through these precious days on Earth.

Human beings are obligated to help other human beings by the simple fact that we exist together. Business with its great power of wealth and global reach can no longer turn the other cheek to its vital contribution to a more humane and balanced world. Does business really have a responsibility to anything or anyone beyond its own profits? No, not technically and perhaps not even legally. Nor do any of us, technically. But morally, ethically and spiritually? That is a very different matter.

◆

Lesson 9

The spiritual purpose of business is to serve the community that supports it

"To be a great company today, you also have to be good company."

JEFFREY IMMELT
FORTUNE 500 CEO

*The spiritual purpose of business is to
serve the community that supports it*

BUSINESS often operates under the mistaken belief that the community it belongs to and is sustained by is there only to serve its needs. Often there is little recognition of its dependence on the community from which it profits. The short-sighted every-man-for-himself approach ignores the fact that people form the foundation of business. Clients and customers serve business by supplying its profits. It is a two-way street, however. In practical and spiritual terms, the purpose of business is to serve the community. When we create a valued product or service, our success is assured.

We need to shift our thinking from business as a parasite or predator to one that is a friend and supporter of the community in which it operates. If we don't, we jeopardize our own welfare. There is strength in our union. Business satisfies the needs of the community and the community rewards business with profit. Together, we are more powerful than apart.

Although money can easily be made through destructive methods, the challenge for spiritually enlightened businesses is to change this dynamic to employ constructive strategies for success. This way, our profits and our souls are in the black. We, in business, have a spiritual obligation to value the community we serve by creating wealth in a socially worthy way. Remember the basic spiritual law: *You are what you do and how you do it.* For years, ruthless or indifferent behavior in business has been acceptable. This concept is ripe for change. All business is part of a greater community. If you adhere to a moral ethic in your personal life, you are honor-bound to include this ethic in your business endeavors.

KEY POINTS IN LESSON NINE

> People form the foundation of business.

> Business is rewarded in profits for serving the needs of the community.

> Business must take responsibility for its role in creating the world around it.

> We have a sacred charge in business to care for the natural world.

HOW DOES LESSON NINE FIT INTO THE BOTTOM LINE?

EXAMPLE #1

PIPE MANUFACTURER

This company's stated "disciplined management practices" include the basic premise of more work for less money. Signs around company plants state the objective is to increase productivity while reducing man hours. Ordinary twenty-first-century workplace comforts are absent. The temperature at production plants can reach over 130 degrees, yet workers toil without air conditioning and managers ration ice cubes for workers. In seven years, 4,600 workers were injured and 9 were killed. Safety of the workforce, judging from its 400 safety violations, isn't a concern at all for company officials. This is more than all its competitors' violations combined. The workforce at this company has a 100% turnover rate. The company has such difficulty hiring local workers that it now recruits mostly ex-convicts. A government official notes that workers are noticeably wounded and disfigured from work-related injuries. Worker safety violations include exposure to dangerous toxins, electrical hazards, unsafe height conditions, damaged machinery and unsafe protection from heated metals. Any worker protections like safety or quality controls were eliminated as being too costly. Clean air and other environmental requirements were also ignored to increase the bottom line.

Company lapses in environmental policy have been called "criminal" by government officials. One plant and its top executives were fined $3 million after falsifying emissions documents. In an unrelated case, other company officials were ordered to do community service, serve three years of probation and pay over $4 million in penalties. They had been convicted of "illegal treatment of hazardous waste and worker safety violations that resulted in the death of an employee."

No matter how many fines or charges the company receives, its profit practices remain unchanged. The habits of "the most dangerous employer in America" are reminiscent of the nineteenth-century industrialists.

The contrasting conditions of competitors reveal that this excessive danger to workers is unnecessary. Another foundry cites worker safety as its top priority and has less than 1% worker turnover per year. It seems at the offending manufacturer, people are literally dying to work there.

EXAMPLE #2

GLOBAL ENERGY COMPANY

This huge conglomerate lists social responsibility as its number-one economic issue. Actions do speak louder than words and the company is acting. It has been touted as a leader of Corporate Social Responsibility in an industry known for its fervent denial of such responsibility. The corporation raises the bar for industry members by actively promoting reduction in greenhouse gases. Rather than "question science, deny responsibility and ignore reality" as they have accused colleagues of doing, top executives are embracing their responsibility and actively searching for solutions. One top exec claims that environmental concerns should serve as an opportunity for innovation, rather than a burden. While other companies spend their money on lobbyists to block environmentally sound legislation, this firm uses it resources to research alternative energy. To this end, the company has launched 300 alternative-energy initiatives. Their goal is a 40% reduction of carbon dioxide in the next few years. They have become the leading developer of solar energy. Their belief is that shareholder value and social responsibility go hand-in-hand.

Employees are motivated by the company's focus on environmental concerns. In all, 60% of the workforce claims the environment is their top priority. Managers are rewarded as much for their ability to reduce emissions as they are for turning a profit. The top executives state that creating non-polluting energy makes "sound business common sense." The chief executive acknowledges the high cost of environmental sustainability, but says that "doing nothing" will cost more. With all the costs of creating environmentally sound energy, this conglomerate earned the same record profits as their environmentally unfriendly contemporaries.

Applying Lesson Nine to Your Life

Business is a community within a larger community. Management influences how employees approach the pursuit of profit. They can choose to work in sync with the larger community they serve and use it as a valuable support system, or they can choose to disrupt the community for their own immediate gain.

Business is not an inanimate object that moves at its own momentum. We speak about business in the third person and explain its direction as if the bottom line had a mind of its own. In reality, people are business. The mind of business is made up of its executives, corporate officers, employers, owners and employees who make decisions for it.

Tools to Include Community Service in Your Business

›   Preserving the environment and our communities serves our own needs as we protect the needs of others.

›   Value the sacred creation of nature.

›   Honor your human obligation to support the greater community as you go about your business.

Creating a Vision of Community

Cherish nature from which you and all else are derived. In the quest for profits, do not separate yourself from your environment. You are in a symbiotic relationship with all that surrounds you. It is possible for you to simultaneously create wealth while contributing to the community you serve. By doing so, you profit both economically and spiritually.

◆

"A human being experiences himself,
his thoughts and feelings, as
something separated from the rest—
a kind of optical illusion of his
consciousness. This illusion is a
prison for us, restricting us to our
personal desires and to affection for
only the few people nearest us. Our
task must be to free ourselves from
this prison by widening our circle
of compassion to embrace all living
beings and all of nature."

ALBERT EINSTEIN

PHYSICIST

A New Era: Fair-Market Capitalism

IF anyone had any doubt that we are all connected, those doubts were erased with the explosion of the World Wide Web in 1995. Suddenly everything we did mattered to everyone else. One end of the world was just a click of the mouse away from another. What you do, what I do, what others do directly affects everyone else through the invisible threads of space and time that create the Internet. Our computer screens manifest in material terms what we already are in the infinite screen of the universe—connected. Every time we read a book, watch a movie, listen to a great piece of music or close our eyes to dream, space and time are transcended by our joint human experience and we meet each other there. Where? In the deepest part of our minds and hearts that is the soul.

This is what happens when we experience human tragedy whether as participant or witness. We become one in our shared suffering. On September 11, 2001 a miraculous moment took place in the midst of our pain. People all over the country, all over the continent and all over the world experienced the pain and horror together. We transcended the isolation of our everyday realities and felt a deep concern for each other. It was a love that went far beyond ordinary loves. It was the love of humanity for one another. Every time we witness human suffering like we did on that day, we gasp the breath of heartache that is shared by all. In those moments, we are carried away by an overwhelming sense of compassion. It is compassion that connects us all.

A friend once said she didn't know why she cried in movies since she never shed a tear in "real" life. In our lives we have many defenses to keep, many guards to maintain just to protect us and help us get through the day. When we witness a powerful human experience either through film or television, our hearts are open because we do not fear the one-dimensional figures on the screen. We feel their emotions because at the very root of our being is the universal human heart that feels love for all. The same happens in tragedy—our separateness is ripped away and we are able to feel our mutual anguish. Like the invisible cords of the Internet across the globe we are corded to each other through our humanness. We reflect what we forgot some time in our infancy, that we are truly connected through one spirit. When I hurt you, I am really hurting myself. Your anguish becomes my own. And so is mine, yours. In our business world, although the same web of connection exists, we often deny or ignore it.

Unfettered Capitalism

Unfettered capitalism, like anything else that lacks a human conscience, needs clear parameters. The view that business has no purpose other than money is another way of claiming that it is not "personal." This translates to "I do not owe you an explanation for what I do in my pursuit of money. Anything I do as long as it's legal is acceptable. I will let the law be my conscience." The Soviet dissident and Nobel Prize winner, Alexander Solzhenitsyn, spoke of the need to go beyond the law: "A society with no other scale but the legal one is not quite worthy of man." At one point in our history, owning human beings was legal. At another point, assaulting your wife was legal. Through the nineteenth century, children as young as nine years old were legally denied schooling and forced to labor along side grown-ups. It was perfectly legal to for people to work in dangerous conditions without clean water, heat, fresh air, fire protection or worker safety conditions of any kind. In the early 1920s, a sign on the window of a Lower East Side New York business read, "If you don't plan to work on Sunday, then don't plan to come in on Monday." These things offer clear proof that laws do not safeguard us from unconscionable human actions.

To serve our higher purpose in modern business by simply "following the rule of law" is not enough. Traditional capitalism's "anything goes in the pursuit of money" philosophy is a relic of the past, a thought process that represents a more primitive aspect of our conscience. Can anyone still justify this in our modern world? A January 20, 2005 issue of British business journal *The Economist* did just that when a journalist claimed that purposeful social responsibility by a corporation does not benefit owners or the public, and can even be harmful. Although four months later another *Economist* writer detailed the "social contract" of business, this issue reveals that some in the financial community continue to endorse self-interest as standard operating procedure.

The same rationale holds true for anyone who has little conscience about how their actions affect other human beings. If we read a defense of slavery in eighteenth- and nineteenth-century America, its viewpoint would be absolutely logical. Ordinary people in early America called slaves "an important part of our property." Others insisted that owning slaves was a "rational right of freedom." Slave traders, slave owners, brutal industrialists and human predators of all kinds explain their indifferent and monstrous abuses very reasonably and simply.

The bone-chilling logic behind some of the twentieth century's most horrifying tragedies reveal that human beings can rationalize anything. Logic without conscience has been human history's greatest enemy.

INTANGIBLE ASSETS

There is nothing tangible about what makes a person charge into a burning building and risk their own life to save yours. Something indefinable motivates them—commitment, duty, perhaps love for humankind. These are the intangibles that make up our life and give it meaning. No matter how hard human beings try, we can never put on paper all that we are. We can never read a history book, scientific explanation, medical analysis or psychological evaluation and have a full picture of what makes a human being tick. There are so many factors in the human mind and heart that transcend our ordinary measures of action—factors deep and indescribable that enable us to love others selflessly, and defy all preconceived logic to the contrary.

The unchecked self-interest long claimed as the foundation for capitalism emanates from our baser human self—the self that hungers to satisfy only its immediate desires. Our higher self is not defined as easily because therein lay the intangibles. The part of ourselves that is moved by the grief of others, that causes us to stop as danger surrounds us and reach out a hand to a complete stranger, the inner self that strives to do the right thing over our own needs. Our conscience, our soul, whatever you choose to call it, is undeniable. We try and try again in our logical ways, but we can never predict how we or anyone else will react under extraordinary circumstances.

In tragedy, ordinary people who have never done anything extraordinary before find themselves performing acts of unimaginable bravery. At the root of all of us exists something greater than we know. Those of us who are moved by the suffering of complete strangers prove this to be true. To insist that we are only interested in ourselves is to claim that we are less than we really are. We are extraordinary beings in an extraordinary world capable of things we haven't yet conceived of. The world of human beings continually surprises and inspires us. Some days are painful and other days are hopeful.

Each of us must reach into our hearts and discover the depth of ourselves beyond what we know. It matters how we do what we do. It matters how we treat others who live in our world. It matters that, like our firefighters, there are people who exist that would give their lives to save us. Without them, we might not even be here. This is the unseen web of connection that everything is built on.

Business is the physical manifestation of our connection to each other. The great illusion of business is the belief that we are separate from one another. This enables us to deceive others, steal from them or otherwise exploit them. Yet our firefighters know innately what many of us forget, that none of us could truly survive without each other.

On September 11, we recognized society's silent foundation of individuals who care for us everyday, people we had never noticed in such a way before. Firefighters, police, doctors, nurses, the people who clean up our garbage to the people that construct our homes—everyone we depend on for our very existence. Business, as it was attacked that day in the air and in New York, was not just some self-serving machine gobbling up victims in its path; it was human beings in service to one another. There isn't much that is more personal than that.

In the immediate aftermath of the tragedy, faced with extreme hatred and violence, our first thoughts were not violent but compassionate. It happened during the tsunami of 2004, and again during Hurricane Katrina. It happens every time we hear of a child being hurt or a family destroyed or any other human tragedy our world endures. This is what we are made of at our deepest most unguarded level: love, not hatred; compassion, not self-interest.

The Business of Making Money

On a morning talk show in the spring of 2006, an oil company executive defended his company's enormous profits against the growing public insurgency regarding high gas prices. When asked if he would "lower profits to help people out," the seasoned CEO responded, "I'm in the business to make money." The implication was clear: his job was to make money, not to help people. This CEO is simply playing by the rules of the game. His public company has done a good job for its corporate executives and shareholders.

However, the difference between his view and the general public is startling. Those with vested interest in his profits see him as a responsible business leader. Others who do not share this interest see him as a monster. His apathy seems to say he does not care enough about the people directly affected. His defense and denial of responsibility only antagonize his customers, because essentially everyone who pulls up to the gas pump has a stake in that company.

In regard to the public duty of corporate executives we are at an impasse. In 1923, former General Motors President Arthur Sloan uttered the famous axiom, "The business of business is business." Almost a century later, the oil CEO's dismissal of social responsibility reveals that some corporate officers still do not understand that business is people. Business is not social work and does not have a charitable mission built into it. But it must have a conscience: a moral one, a social one, and a spiritual one. Business has a soul because all those who are in it have a soul. It does not owe its public a free ride, but it does owe them a fair deal.

Appropriate questions for a responsible money manager might be "Shouldn't you offer your customers a quality product at an affordable price? And do you think it is reasonable to harm people in the process of making a profit?" Lowering profits to be fair to consumers is simply part of the cost of doing business. Factor this cost into your bottom line and you won't feel like you are losing money. Treat it as an expense, because in reality, it is.

The public can't boycott gasoline. It is a basic staple of modern life. Therefore buying gas is not a free exchange but a forced exchange. If a consumer cannot exercise freedom of choice over a commodity their livelihood depends on, different rules apply. In all the rhetoric about protecting the rights of business, we forget that the free market system works both ways. Business has a right to free enterprise, but so does the consumer. Hiking gasoline prices to materially damaging levels interferes with the basic freedom of the American consumer. The key issue for any company selling an essential product is that the nature of its business is public service.

The Price of Greed

As profit-driven capitalists, we are wary of overregulation by government officials who hold office for limited years and have little business expertise. The Sarbanes-Oxley Act, created to curtail corporate deception, is thought by many modern corporations to be a poorly devised bureaucratic mess. Perhaps its efficiency could be improved, however its necessity is very real. Some corporate executives at Enron, WorldCom, Tyco and several other large public companies who could not regulate themselves forced the government to step in between the company assets and their individual appetites for greed. Their gluttony posed a public threat to our nation's economy.

It is not a new story, but an old story stretching far back into antiquity. Over and over, those who could, gained their wealth and power at the expense of those who could not defend themselves. From the Holy Roman Empire to feudal times, the French and English monarchs, the czars of Russia, the robber barons of our Gilded Age right through to Ivan Boesky and Bernie Ebbers of our current world—history is filled with examples like this. And history is also full of stories of people who took the excessive greed of their rulers into their own hands. The revolutions of France, Russia and our own exemplify the power of the public over exploitation.

We stand on the threshold of yet another revolution: the transition of dog-eat-dog, survival-of-the-fittest capitalism to the establishment of "free and fair" market capitalism. We like to think of ourselves as free market capitalists who value free enterprise. Our capitalistic structure fits into our natural concepts of personal liberty. Everyone has the opportunity to create their own fortune; that is the American way. Only not on the backs of others; that is not the American way. As our founding fathers wrote in their inimitable foresight, "All men are created equal." However, if we are part of the corporate executive hierarchy, as opposed to the lower economic level of workers, then we are not equal.

But our forefathers' wisdom prepared for this. Their noble thoughts surpassed even their own actions. We will probably never be born equal in terms of economics or advantages, yet Americans believe our founders clearly meant that all men and women should be answerable to the same laws and have access to the same opportunities. In our corporate world this dynamic does not always exist. The system is set up so executives of publicly traded companies can reap the benefits of other people's money and not answer for it. The board of directors is an incestuous and autonomous entity that makes crucial financial decisions without the input of investors. The frustration with corporate structure is that unlike anywhere else in our beautifully democratic society, public corporations often resemble the old monarchies of Europe more than they do our own system.

Why shouldn't our publicly traded companies be run on the principles of democracy and fair play that we profess to value? Although we are told it is very "complicated," in reality it's simpler than we think. If you want to be a public corporation and reap all the subsequent benefits, then you must answer to the public.

CONSCIENCE AS OUR GUIDE

Philosopher Albert Schweitzer said, "The first step in the evolution of ethics is a sense of solidarity with other human beings." Is the oil CEO a monster? Probably not. He's probably just an ordinary man who values our free market system and believes in the rules of the game such as they are. Not a monster, just a businessman without a sense of solidarity to other human beings who do not share his interests.

We cannot always teach old dogs new tricks, but we can take action for ourselves. When economic indifference affects our lives directly, we must speak up and name the injustice. When asked about social responsibility, modern business can no longer answer, "It's not my job," and not look irresponsible.

It might be difficult for some who have operated for decades under the old rules to learn the new. It was a process for British Loyalists in our nation's infancy to accept a land without a king. It was a process for slavemasters to understand they had no right to own other human beings. It was a process for early industrialists to discover their basic obligations to the workforce. It was a process for segregationists to allow equal opportunity for minorities and women. So too is it a process for us to include a sense of responsibility to others in our 200-year-old capitalism.

This brings us to the purpose of *spiritual capitalism*. Bringing the spirit and conscience of each of us into our pursuit of money is what modern business requires. We need to add logic with conscience to our capitalism. Following the law is not enough to create principled wealth. Ethical conscience infused into free market capitalism becomes *fair-market capitalism.*

An American Dream

On September 11, 2001, our American dream shattered. The results of years of hard work and sacrifice were gone in the course of a day. No longer did we feel insulated from human suffering. No more could we hide behind the shelter of our affluence. As the Towers fell, so did our innocence. Suddenly we were part of a greater scheme than our exclusive world had allowed. The blessings we took for granted and the privileges we enjoyed were destroyed in moments. The world's anguish had landed on our doorstep and we could no longer look the other way.

The attack of 9/11 will remain one of the pivotal events of our century. Whatever unfolds in the years to come, the story of our millennium will always begin with this event and its ripples throughout the modern world. We personally witnessed it through a particular lens—the heroes and victims who lived and died through it. With that view, we saw ourselves as part of a larger plan. The American dream had shattered for many of us. As Americans, we always felt ourselves to be "keepers of the flame"—the flame of liberty. We protected the weak, righted the world's wrongs and championed the helpless. Suddenly we were made responsible for things over which we had no control, nor even any knowledge of. Our victims were innocent as they sat unknowing in their airplane seats and the chairs of their desks. Our saviors knew not the hateful machines that were to devour them.

It was said that *we* were responsible. But responsible for what? Politics in a far-off land? The slaughter of innocents we never knew? A religious fanaticism that held no personal connection or logic? An inexplicable hatred that cut through time and space to disrupt our peace?

The World Trade Center, New York City, the United States of America. Rich, richer and richest. There was an enemy among us and it was ourselves. Our wealth and power made us targets for the ills of the world. Our firefighters and those who were tragically unlucky to be in the way paid the price for us all.

As the vicious killers took our beloveds, we asked, "Why?" We watched the international news and were astounded to see hundreds of people dancing in the streets to our destruction. We heard the grumblings throughout the continents that we "deserved it," quietly at first, then louder. The arrogant and privileged America had finally taken a fall. Ordinary people in far-off places smiled with secret satisfaction, declaring, "I couldn't help but think they got what they deserved." It was not just the hatred of the depraved, it was the bitterness of the ordinary too. We were mystified. Why would any caring, thinking person feel justified in the murders of innocents? We were told again we were responsible. But responsible for what?

As we rebuilt our world and mended our dream throughout the next year, murmurs of our indifference to the pain of others surfaced. Middle Eastern news shows reported it, European newspapers wrote of it. America was the cause of its own demise. *Us?* Americans? Champions of the underdog indifferent to the suffering of others? We are compassionate, honorable people. Didn't they know that? Didn't they know that America is *everyone*? We are the "tired," the "poor," the "huddled masses yearning to be free." That is what our country is built on. In our land of cherished freedom, everyone had been welcome. Our diversity was the glue that bound us together and made us great. Now we questioned that—the very foundation of our society.

In the year that followed, it was revealed that America has an image of arrogance throughout much of the world. Our wealth is viewed as protection from what others endure daily. The engine that drives us, American capitalism, has been called ruthless and vicious. Yet most of us have suffered greatly to be here. Those who were brought here in chains, those whose lands were stolen or destroyed, those who pioneered in dangerous conditions, the persecuted who flocked here, the brave who escaped poverty and war and risked everything to flee oppression and pursue their dreams... America knows suffering. Our nation was founded on it.

The Enemy Within

On that bloody September morning, we were accused of being indifferent to the suffering of others as a small group of militants were indifferent to ours. A tit for tat, an eye for an eye. How did we deserve such retaliation? Had we hurt anyone, starved anyone, imprisoned anyone?

It was discovered that our money was the enemy, not only to the tyrants that engineered the attack, but to the ordinary people who applauded it. Our affluence gave the illusion of indifference. Our comforts and ease made us seem impenetrable.

America's wealth was viewed as the root of all evil. Business was its public face and therefore held responsible. But we asked again, responsible for what? This time we knew. Business with its impersonal façade was charged with gross negligence for human suffering. Had it caused it? No, probably not. But its apathy and denial of human anguish made it the target for misdirected rage.

After September 11, business could no longer hide from itself. We could no longer remain behind the anonymity of our corporate veil. The veil had been lifted. We were exposed. The corporation was us, human beings with faces and real needs like everyone else. Wall Street was not a place, but a community of people that stretched around the world. Our humanness was revealed for all to see.

The Drive to Make Money

Capitalism has created wealth for the largest amount of people ever in recorded history. All we need to do is look around America to confirm this. Our nation was built on hundreds of millions of people throwing off centuries of history and reinventing themselves. A nation of mavericks and entrepreneurs, American optimism gets us out of bed in the morning and gives us hope for a better life. Our "rugged individualism" has been the catalyst for our affluence. However, it has also encouraged our separateness.

None of us are truly separate from the other in our essential human experience. In tragedy, we not only see our connections, but also our equality. We long for loved ones, feel afraid, and pray for help. Income and wealth have little importance in the moments of our lives where only life and love matter. Harvard Business School professor Scotty McLennan tells students, "People on their deathbeds often say the only thing that mattered about their lives was the amount of love they'd given and received." This is because human beings are so much more than money. Tragedies prove that we are made of intangibles like courage, honor and love as much as greed, selfishness and hate. These characteristics cannot be discounted in our quest for profit.

Capitalism that claims no personal responsibility to other human beings is fundamentally flawed. Making money is not our only conscious purpose. Our need for money often emanates from love for our families or our wish to be recognized and appreciated. We use money as protection from being humiliated, abandoned or invisible. We strive to be secure in an unpredictable world. There are many unseen emotional factors behind our drive for money. Thinking and feeling people find the impersonal myth of business inadequate. *We* are business.

STRIKING A BALANCE

The time has come for us to leave behind the arrogant image of pure self-interest and include our higher selves in our pursuit of profit. As businesspeople, we can see our part in the greater plan as clearly as a firefighter because we understand that business is a service to others. We are only the stewards of that service.

Whether you believe in a transcendent God, a human God or no God at all, your personal spirit infuses everything you do. It is this spirit to be better, to push beyond our own expectations that drives us. Capitalism is not a finished product. It evolves in the same way as any of us do individually. In our new millennium, we are poised to improve. There is a balance to be struck between self-interest and altruism.

Spiritual capitalism is not about giving money away, it is about how we make it in relation to the world around us. Our pursuit of profit involves more than basic economics, management methods or the superficial logic of supply and demand. It goes beyond regulations, laws and corporate responsibility right down to the essence of who we are. In our collective spirit, we make decisions in our money affairs the same way we decide anything else in our lives—with a clear recognition of our personal duty to others.

WHO ARE WE IN BUSINESS?

These are the final questions for modern capitalism: Who are we in business? Are we predators or people with a conscience? Do we value the sacredness of human life, or not? In the preceding chapters we have given examples of hugely profitable companies and enormously wealthy individuals who created their success while including compassion and conscience. We have detailed the fundamental concepts of the higher spiritual truth for all to ponder. In the end it comes down to each of us individually. You must answer for yourself the overriding question: who are you in business?

As the sentence of Jeffrey Skilling, ex-chief executive of Enron, is handed down in the fall of 2006, five years after the attack on our nation, the irony is not lost on us. We wonder if any law would have stopped him or the late Kenneth Lay in their greed. Perhaps as they profited at the expense of others, they did not think beyond their own needs. Perhaps they did not care about the suffering they caused. Perhaps they never gave it a thought. The militants on September 11 clearly did not feel any solidarity with us as human beings. Nor did the Enron executives seem to feel any solidarity with employees, shareholders or the greater economic community.

Nor do many individuals in the business community share a sense of connection with those outside their scope, because for centuries, those of us in business have been taught not to. It has become ingrained in us. "It's not personal, it's business" has been repeated so many times, we have come to believe it. How many of us never questioned that edict? How much suffering has that one simple statement caused humanity? It is time to unlearn the myths we have inherited. The business of business is people.

A major component missing in the human system of economics is the spirituality behind our pursuit of profit. The detached posture we have adopted in our standard profit practices is indicative of a less-developed mindset. We do not leave our personal selves out of our business activities. Whether we are aware of it or not our conscience and connection to others comes with us wherever we go. Rather than denying this part of ourselves, we must activate it. Harvard MBA and a professor at Boston University, Jennifer F. Lawrence says, "Spirituality should not be confused with 'religion.' To me, spirituality is simply having a sense of inner calm and a willingness to reflect carefully on yourself and the world around you." We must reflect on the world around us and consider how our behavior affects others if we are people with a conscience. The predators will always be here, but the vast majority of us can create a powerful force of capitalism with a conscience that renders them insignificant.

A Sacred Charge

Like our firefighters and every other member of the helping community, we have a sacred charge in business. The job of firefighters is to put out fires and respond to emergencies to the best of their ability. Saving lives at the risk of their own goes beyond their job description, yet this is what they do every day. After the tragedy, we were personally humbled by their selflessness. For us, the guiding principle of self-interest in business no longer seemed adequate. We saw our purpose in business as something greater than ourselves. There is an unspoken agreement that goes beyond our job description of making money and increasing the bottom line. Like a firefighter whose duty it is to protect and preserve lives, ours is to protect and preserve livelihoods. Every time we take money from a client or customer we make a commitment that our product is worthy. Every employee we hire, every community we operate in is due our respect and consideration. This is the sacred contract behind our work.

Business is about generating profit. It is also about service. Business profits because it serves. Yet business without a soul is as empty as any of us would be without one. By opening the heart in business, we create a new capitalism worthy of our modern era, a spiritual capitalism that uses the pursuit of money to enhance the world around us.

What is *spiritual* capitalism? It is the personal side of our pursuit of profit. We are no longer a corporation, company, business, executive, manager, CEO, CFO, employer or employee. We are human beings operating in the world of profit and money to benefit ourselves and those we serve. Spiritual capitalism goes beyond our profit margins and penetrates our hearts and minds. We can no longer hide behind the detached façade of business because we understand it really is personal for all of us. It requires a shift of conscience to occur within *us*, not just the institutions in which we operate.

Spiritual capitalism is not for the weak minded. It is for hearty, visionary mavericks like our early countrymen who don't perceive any challenge as too great. We see our deeper values as worth fighting for. To achieve this high ideal we need to be bold, take risks and push beyond our own limits. Retired FDNY Captain Al Fuentes, who survived the Towers crashing down on him, tells students at John Jay College in New York that as they work for money they should also "leave the world a better place." To be worthy of our sacred contract, we must include this view in our pursuit of profit. In our business community, there are blazing fires of corruption, greed and indifference. Just like a firefighter, we must put them out.

◆

"When you cease to make a contribution, you begin to die."

ELEANOR ROOSEVELT

FIRST LADY

Postscript

JULY 2006

The future of business depends upon a simple shift in thinking, from an exclusive sense of self to an inclusive sense of the whole. It all starts within.

In the four and a half years since this tragic event and the two years since we completed the first edition of this book, things have changed in New York. Wall Street is booming again. Investment banks and financial firms are posting record profits. New York real estate has doubled in value since September 2001, despite a year-long slowdown. Our headhunting firm is back to pre-9/11 levels of business. We have kept many old clients and developed new ones. Our real estate investments are performing well. Business and our lives are back to normal. Or are they?

In January 2004, we discussed the attack with several business associates who were severely affected by 9/11. The group included an attorney from a large downtown law firm, the president of a commercial building design company formerly near One World Trade Center, a senior director at a midtown advertising firm, the CEO of a midtown financial services firm and a lieutenant in the New York City Fire Department. All five echoed the sentiment of many of our colleagues on Wall Street, in other industries and the FDNY: "These have been the worst two years of my life."

They were for us too. Two of the worst years of our lives, as we saw many of our friends perish and those who didn't, suffer deeply. We personally lost millions of dollars in revenues and saw our city's landscape and ease permanently changed. Our beloved friend, New York City Firefighter Mark, was forced to resign at the age of forty-three due to severely reduced lung capacity, a direct result of the poisonous air at Ground Zero.

Firefighters from 9/11 continue to struggle daily with the enormous physical and psychological ailments they incurred from the attack. Many First Responders suffer from cancer, respiratory diseases and terminal illnesses from their dedication at Ground Zero, and receive surprisingly little help from government agencies.

Our nation went to war, Wall Street and the business community became embroiled in scandals, America's innocence and compassion turned to hatred and fear. We lost so much in a precious short period of time.

From the vantage point of our reclaimed comfort, our view has been indelibly imprinted. We watch now the people of Mississippi, New Orleans, the earthquake-ravaged mountains of Pakistan, the victims of human and natural tragedies all over the world suffer as we did four years ago and as many others did before us. The people of New Orleans still don't have homes or a city. Their entire history was wiped out when the levees broke. Our hearts go out to them in their time of need. Their suffering is ours. We know some of what they are going through. Even more, we have an idea of the challenges they will face in the next few years.

What heartens us most through these tragedies are the heroic and extraordinary ways that Americans and friends around the world jump in to offer their help, hands and homes. These events confirm that we are kind, caring people. It renews our faith in each other once more. We have seen that at the heart of each of us is compassion and goodness.

Extreme events in our lives are inevitable. Nobody escapes them. Tragedies like 9/11 happen every day. Natural disasters, human-made disasters, wars, serious illnesses and the loss of loved ones or life as we know it, these are all 9/11s. When they occur, painful as they are, they serve as opportunities for transformation. There is always something important to learn from them. Why did it happen? Could it have been avoided? How did we react to it? What does it teach us about ourselves and those around us?

Living through the middle of an historical event of mammoth proportions on September 11, 2001 taught us two important things. Firstly, that there is more *good* in the world than *bad*. While a small group of people planned our demise and celebrated our misery, the vast majority of the human world suffered with us. Secondly, we understand our duty is to remind people of that simple truth and to share our renewed faith in humanity with anyone who will listen. We survived the attack personally and collectively from our own strength, combined with the compassion and assistance of millions of others.

Thank you all for giving us hope when we needed it most. We will never forget.

—Monika and Peter Ressler

Nine Spiritual Lessons of Business

LESSON ONE

BUSINESS IS PERSONAL

- › Everything you do in business is personal to someone.

- › The claim that business is not personal is a deliberate deception.

- › *Responsibility-of-the-fittest* must replace *survival-of-the-fittest*.

LESSON TWO

USE YOUR PURSUIT OF MONEY AS A TOOL FOR GOOD

- › When we exchange money for goods or services we create a sacred covenant with each other.

- › Money is not a thing that controls you—you control it.

- › *Good* is that which enhances, *evil* is that which destroys.

Lesson Three

Profit honorably without taking from others

- ‣ Gain at the expense of others is not a worthy "win."

- ‣ The suffering you create for others and yourself is unnecessary suffering.

- ‣ A genuine sense of security is based on personal character.

Lesson Four

Giving to others is a gift for yourself

- ‣ The nature of your actions reverberates into the world and returns to you.

- ‣ Concern for others is concern for yourself.

- ‣ When you include others in your view, your world expands.

- ‣ Business needs to give because it takes.

Lesson Five

You serve others through the intelligent design of work

- ‣ The spiritual purpose of work is to serve each other.

- ‣ Every job is a helping profession.

- ‣ All jobs have equal spiritual value.

- ‣ There is an intelligent design behind our work that binds us together.

Lesson Six

Calculate the human cost into the bottom line

- Business has a responsibility to those it affects.

- Capitalism must include the human factor in its calculations.

- The ultimate bottom line is life itself.

Lesson Seven

The foundation of business is trust

- Hard work and creative ingenuity equal good business— not deception.

- We create trust by establishing positive relationships with customers, suppliers, our workforce and clients.

- Money is the by-product of our business efforts, but relationships are the essence.

- Repeat business and referrals are what we strive for.

Lesson Eight

Teamwork is the heart of business

- The workplace is a sacred place as it is a manifestation of human existence.

- Management must create, communicate and inspire employees to a shared vision.

- Employers and employees form a spiritual partnership.

Lesson Nine

The spiritual purpose of business is to serve the community that supports it

> People form the foundation of business.

> Business is rewarded in profits for serving the needs of the community.

> Business must take responsibility for its role in creating the world around it.

> We have a sacred charge in business to care for the natural world.

◆

Nine Ways to Practice Spiritual Capitalism

1. Remember that everything you do in business is personal to someone.

2. Use your pursuit of money to improve the lives of others as you improve your own.

3. Don't lose sight of the people and things that are most important to you in your pursuit of money.

4. Understand that life is a reciprocal cycle—in order to receive you need to give.

5. Think of your work as a service to others and value the work of others for their contribution to you.

6. Consider the consequences of your money decisions on others before you act on them.

7. Be true in your word and deed in your business dealings.

8. Remember your employers, employees, clients, customers and suppliers are your business partners.

9. Cherish the world around you through your work and business.

Notes on Sources

Most of the information in this manuscript was derived from personal experiences, conversations and observations through two decades of business activity. See below for other sources that were used for quotes or facts.

The Roots of Spiritual Capitalism

Atack, Jeremy and Peter Passell. *A New Economic View of American History*. W.W. Norton & Company, 1994.

Colvin, Geoff, "100 Best Companies To Work For." *Fortune*, January 23, 2006.

Friedman, Milton. "The Social Responsibility of Business is to Increase Its Profits." *New York Times*, September 13, 1970.

Gunther, Marc. "God and Business." *Fortune*, July 9, 2001.

Heilbroner, Robert and Aaron Singer. *The Economic Transformation of America, 1600 to Present*. Harcourt Brace & Company, 1999.

Hughes, Jonathan and Louis Cain. *American Economic History*. Pearson Education, 2003.

Josephson, Matthew. *The Robber Barons*. Harcourt, Inc., 1962.

Loomis, Carol. "Warren Buffett Gives It Away." *Fortune*, July 10, 2006.

Smith, Adam. *The Wealth of Nations*. Bantam/Dell Edition, 2003.

Chapter 2: Money: The Root of All Evil?

"Economy: It's bad, but not for long." *Crain's*, December 10, 2001.

Fredrickson, Tom. "City Lost 79,000 Jobs In October." *NewYorkBusiness.com*, November 16, 2001.

Chapter 3: An American Tragedy

Ackman, Dan. "Bernie Ebbers Guilty." *Forbes*, March 15, 2005.

Brush, Michael. "CEOs cut pensions, pad their own." *MSNMoney.com*, January 18, 2006.

CNN Money. "America's CEO: 'I'm sorry.'" April 22, 2003.

Colvin, Geoffrey. "Targeting CEO Comp." *Fortune*, December 12, 2005.

Crawford, Kristen. "Ex-Tyco CEO Kozlowski found guilty." *CNNMoney.com*, June 21, 2005.

Dignan, Larry. "Fiorina: 10,000 layoffs by Nov. 1" *News.com*, July 4, 2002.

Dow Jones/AP. "Fed Official Wants Executives' Pay Cut." *New York Times*, September 12, 2002.

Farrell, Greg. "Ebbers' luck runs out in sweeping victory for feds." *USA Today*, March 16, 2005.

Fortier, Mark. "Former Telecom CEO Leo Hindery on CEO Responsibilities, Pay, and Ethics." *FrugalMarketing.com*, 2006.

Gardner, Nancy. "Profit-driven corporations can make management blind to ethics, study says." *UW Business School News*, January 9, 2006.

Greenspan, Alan. "FRB Testimony: Monetary policy report to the Congress." *www.federalreserve.gov/boarddocs*, July 16, 2002.

Kandel, Myron. "CEO Pay: Tighten The Screws." *CNN Money*, April 25, 2003.

Lublin, Joann S. "A Few Share the Wealth." *Wall Street Journal*, December 12, 2005.

McGee, Marianne Kolbasuk. "HP Sued Over Ex-CEO Fiorina's $42 Million Severance Payout." *Information Week*, March 7, 2006.

Mulligan, Thomas S. "Lawyer for Skilling Spars With Fastow." *Los Angeles Times*, March 8, 2006.

Murphy, Kate. "Corporate Lepers, Local Heroes?" *BusinessWeek*, June 30, 2005.

Rather, Dan. "The Great Inventor." *60 Minutes II*, August 27, 2003.

Strauss, Gary and Barbara Hansen. "Special report: CEO pay 'business as usual.'" *USA Today*, March 30, 2005.

Weiss, Gary, Paula Dwyer, and Mara Der Hovanesian. "Big Changes for the Big Board." *BusinessWeek*, September 18, 2003.

Chapter 4: The Miracle

Blum, Justin and Jeffrey Birnbaum. "On Profit and Pump Prices." *Washington Post*, November 10, 2005.

Fuentes, Alfredo. *American By Choice*. Fire Dreams Publishing Co., 2004.

Whitfield, Fredericka. "Interview with Kimeli Nalyyomah." *CNN Sunday Morning*, June 9, 2002.

Chapter 6: The Human Bottom Line

Associated Press. "Senators Vent on Oil Company Executives." *FOXNews.com*, November 9, 2005.

Associated Press. "Wal-Mart seeking global ethics chief." *MSNBC. MSN.com*, March 3, 2006.

Bashinsky, Ruth. "Bravest Team Saves Four." *Daily News*, February 21, 2003.

Byrne, John A. "The Faces of the Jobless Recovery." *Fast Company*, April 2004.

Colvin, Geoffrey. "America Isn't Ready (Here's What to Do About It)." *Fortune*, July 25, 2005.

Engardio, Peter with Michael Arndt and Dean Foust. "The Future of Outsourcing." *BusinessWeek*, January 30, 2006.

Friedman, Thomas, *The World Is Flat*. Farrar, Straus and Giroux, 2005.

Flynn, Kevin. "2 more firefighters arrested in dispute on search for bodies." *New York Times*, November 6, 2001

Greenhouse, Steven. "How Costco Became the Anti-Wal-Mart." *New York Times*, July 17, 2005.

Greenhouse, Steven and Michael Barbaro. "Wal-Mart Memo Suggests Ways to Cut Employee Benefit Costs." *New York Times*, October 26, 2005.

Hebert, Josef H. "Oil Company Execs Defend Profits to Senate." *Washington Post*, November 10, 2005.

Maclay, Kathleen. "UC Berkeley study assesses 'second wave' of outsourcing U.S. jobs." *NewsCenter.Berkeley.edu*, October 29, 2003.

Ouimet, J-Robert. *The Golden Book*. Holding O.C.B. Inc. & Ouimet-Tomasso, Inc., 2005.

Reingold, Jennifer. "A Brief (Recent) History of Offshoring," "Into Thin Air," "The Responsibility to Retrain." *Fast Company*, April 2004.

Saul, Michael. "Firehouse closings are cool, panel sez." *Daily News*, April 9, 2003.

Chapter 7: An Absence of Trust

Associated Press. "Rights group says Yahoo gave China information used to jail a third Chinese user." *USA Today*, April 19, 2006.

Associated Press. "Enron 'Mastermind' Pleads Guilty." *CBSNews.com*, October 17, 2002.

Bergin, Mark. "The Great Firewall." *World Magazine*, March 25, 2006.

Brady, Diane, Marcia Vickers with Mike McNamee. "AIG: What Went Wrong." *BusinessWeek*, April 11, 2005.

Befus, Lauren and Danielle McGillis. "Electrolux leaving Greenville." *Daily News*, January 16, 2004.

Enron Corporation. "Enron's 1998 Annual Report, 'Our Values.'" *www.som.yale.edu/faculty/Sunder*, 2005.

Floyd, Nell Luter. "A lot of people relied on (Ebbers) for jobs." *USA Today*, March 16, 2005

Gonzales, Vince. "California Energy Crisis A Sham." *CBSNews.com*, September 17, 2002.

Greenspan, Alan. "Commencement address, Wharton School of Business, University of Pennsylvania." *www.federalreserve.gov/boarddocs*, May 15, 2005.

Heilemann, John. "Journey to the (Revolutionary, Evil-Hating, Cash-Crazy, and Possibly Self-Destructive) Center of Google." *GQ*, 2004.

Hymowitz, Carol. "Managers Thrive in Crises By Listening to Dissenters." *CareerJournal.com*, July 2006.

Ignatius, Adi. "In Search of the Real Google." *Time*, February 20, 2006.

Kaufman, Marc. "Merck CEO Resigns as Drug Probe Continues." *Washington Post*, May 6, 2005.

Kirchgaessner, Stephanie. "Internet Giants Grilled on China Policies." *Financial Times*, February 16, 2006.

Morgenson, Gretchen and Jenny Anderson. "MARKET PLACE: The Performance Vanishes." *New York Times*, May 3, 2005.

Thomas, Dave. "Missouri Jury Tells State Farm to Pay." *Insurance Journal*, September 5, 2005.

Chapter 8: All for One and One for All

Bartlett, Donald and James Steele. "The Broken Promise." *Time*, October 23, 2005.

Drucker, Peter. *The Essential Drucker*. Harper Business, 2001.

Fuentes, Alfredo. *American By Choice*. Fire Dreams Publishing Co., 2004.

Fox, Ruediger. "International Spirit At Work Awards." *ASAW*, October 2005.

Glen, Bill. "His work is a precious place." *Western Catholic Reporter*, February 13, 2006.

Greenleaf, Robert. "What is Servant-Leadership." *The Robert K. Greenleaf Center for Servant-Leadership*, 2002.

Gunther, Marc. *Faith and Fortune*. Crown Business, 2004.

Josephson, Matthew. *The Robber Barons*. Harcourt, Inc., 1962.

Labich, Kenneth. "Is Herb Kelleher America's Best CEO?" *Fortune*, May 2, 1994.

Lincoff, Audrey. "Starbucks and the National Labor Relations Board Enter into Settlement Agreement." *Finanzen News*, March 8, 2006.

Nichols, John. "Unionizing Whole Foods Would Be Fitting." *Capital Times*, June 27, 2002.

Schmidt, Eric and Hal Varian. "Google: Ten Golden Rules." *Newsweek*, December 2, 2005.

Wong, Grace. "Kozlowski gets up to 25 years." *CNN.com*, September 19, 2005.

Chapter 9: A Brave New World

Barstow, David and Lowell Bergman. "At a Texas Foundry, An Indifference to Life." *New York Times*, January 8, 2003.

Goodstein, Laurie. "Evangelical Leaders Join Global Warming Initiative." *New York Times*, February 8, 2006.

Gunther, Marc. "Money and Morals at GE." *Fortune*, November 15, 2004.

Gunther, Marc. "Compassionate capitalism at Timberland." *Fortune*, February 8, 2006.

PBS. *Frontline*. "A Dangerous Business," January 9, 2003.

Epilogue: A New Era: Fair-Market Capitalism

Crook, Clive. "The Good Company." *Economist*, January 20, 2005.

Finkelstein, Mark. "Lauer: 'Would Exxon Lower Prices to Help Out in This Time of Need?'" *NewsBusters.org*, May 3, 2006.

Pavia, Jim. "Excessive exec pay symptomatic of weak boards." *Crain's*, March 13, 2006.

Pro-slavery petition in Virginia, 1784. The Library of Virginia.

Rigoglioso, Marguerite. "Spirit at Work: The Search for Deeper Meaning in the Workplace." *Harvard Business School Alumni Bulletin*, April 1999.

Index

About the Authors

PETER RESSLER and MONIKA MITCHELL RESSLER have been life partners and business partners for the past fifteen years. Together they founded one of Wall Street's premier executive search firms, specializing in institutional debt and equity, sales, trading and research. Their clients represent the top tier investment banking firms, global money management firms and commercial banks worldwide.

Cornell University business graduate and twenty-five year Wall Street veteran, Peter Ressler began his career at a large midtown search firm, serving as managing director until he left the firm to start his own in 1995. He is currently the CEO of RMG Search, Inc. and partner-in-charge of the institutional debt and equity division.

Monika Mitchell originally planned to pursue political science and international law. After her parents' untimely death when she was twenty-two, Monika left plans for law school behind and began her professional life as an actress in New York City, gradually moving into playwriting, directing and producing, before becoming a Wall Street recruiter. Monika holds a BA in theatre arts from State University of New York and is currently working on her master's degree in social science at the Maxwell School of Public Administration at Syracuse University. She currently serves as Co-CEO and partner-in-charge of the firm's investment and development division.

The Resslers have been on a lifelong spiritual odyssey. Several years ago, their search culminated in a profound awakening that changed the course of their lives. They have emerged as leaders in the movement for the social and spiritual transformation of business.

After September 11, 2001, Peter became a member of his local volunteer fire department in Islip, New York. He is currently a member of the Lebanon, New Jersey Volunteer Fire Department "FAST" team and the Oldwick, New Jersey Volunteer Fire Department. Monika works with terminally ill patients as a hospice care volunteer and the UMC Mission Committee.

They are members of the Fiver Foundation, the World Business Academy and Companies That Care. They serve on the board of directors of the Association for Spirit at Work.

In the fall of 2004, the Resslers moved their primary residence to rural Tewksbury Township, New Jersey, where they reside with their two boys and two dogs. They divide their time between their New Jersey farm, New York City and Martha's Vineyard.

For further information,

please contact:

SPIRITUAL CAPITALISM
243 Fifth Avenue, #227
New York, NY 10016
Tel: 212-741-1748
Fax: 212-741-8040
info@spiritualcapitalism.com
www.spiritualcapitalism.com

THE RESSLER MITCHELL GROUP –
RMG SEARCH, INC.
Tel: 212-337-1700
www.rmgsearch.com